Too. Hurried To Love

Too Hurried to Love

Living with Simplicity and Purpose

Charles Bradshaw
AND Dave Gilbert

HARVEST HOUSE PUBLISHERS
Eugene, Oregon 97402

TOO HURRIED TO LOVE

Copyright © 1991 by Harvest House Publishers
Eugene, Oregon 97402

Library of Congress Cataloging-in-Publication Data

Bradshaw, Charles, 1948-
      Too hurried to love / Charles Bradshaw, Dave Gilbert.
      ISBN 0-89081-887-8
         1. Christian life—1960—.   2. Interpersonal relations—Religious
      aspects—Christianity.   3. Love—Religious aspects—Christianity.
      I. Gilbert, Dave, 1956-   II. Title.
      BV4501.2.G485   1991   91-9693
      248.4—dc20   CIP

*To our fellow laborers
in the process of giving birth to this book.*

*We love you:
Suzi, Charlotte, Jana, Deb, Amy and Tyler.
Now we have time to play.*

CONTENTS

//

Preface

//

This is a book for people like us. People who enjoy being busy and who want to make an impact on their world. It's just that sometimes we feel like an out-of-control freight train that is still accelerating. In fact, as we progress in life, we have found that life gets more complex and demanding, not less. It's not becoming easier to find time for family or friends, time for solitude or God. The more we talked to people about our struggle to find time for the ones we love, the more confirming comments came back to us strong and clear. "Your struggle is my struggle." "Can you give us any tips?" *Too Hurried to Love* is our attempt to help people live with the pace of our world today.

This is not another book about slowing down. It is about decisive living. That is, living with direction and purpose that accepts our personal limits and understands the motivating forces that work on us. We have written a book to help people change their lifestyle, their thinking, and their behavior in a way that will give them time to love.

Too Hurried to Love is a book that has come through the sieve of our own experience. Throughout most of our adult lives, both of us have been on a search to understand how we might live and be happy in the face of the confusing pace of everyday living in this last half of the twentieth century. This book represents the progress we have made.

Let us encourage you not to skim this book quickly. Our effort has been to cover the subject of being "too hurried to love" with an eye for application. You'll find handles in this book to help you deal with the elusive idea of life focus and balance. Allow yourself to put your fingers between the pages and pause long enough to consider the action steps listed for you at the end of each chapter. In fact, don't just consider the action steps...*do* them. We never intended that this would be a book you'd want to tell others you simply *read*; this is a book you will tell others you *did*.

—Charlie and Dave
Diamond Bar, California

Too. Hurried to Love

1

The Pace of the Race

// ♥

"There is more to life than increasing its speed."

—Tim Hansel

"All my possessions for a moment in time."

—Queen Elizabeth I,
with her dying breath,
1603

This is a book for busy people.

In fact, if you have the time to read this book in one sitting—if you can prop up your feet and read free of distraction and interruption—then it's probably not for you.

However, if you started your day around dawn and are planning to end it sometime after the late-night news...if your day was a blur of appointments, assignments, and deadlines...if you're trying to read this while waiting for a plane, sitting in the back seat of a taxi, helping the kids with their homework, doing the laundry, or riding the exercise bike... to you we say: Read on!

You already know that our world seems to be moving very quickly these days—faster than ever before. And the accelerated pace has probably changed the way you function and even the way you look at things. Most likely, it's changed the way you relate to other people. Some days are so hectic that simply giving another person the time of day feels like an act of charity.

Sometimes the pace of life in our society gives us the feeling of being dragged down the road against our will. It can make us feel a little bit the way a dog named Tattoo must have felt on a certain occasion:

> Tattoo, the basset hound, never intended to go for an evening run, but had no choice when his owner shut his leash in the car door and took off for a drive—with Tattoo still outside the vehicle!
>
> Tacoma [Washington] Police motorcycle officer, Terry Filbert, was driving near North 21st and Adam Street about 7:25 P.M., Wednesday, when he noticed a vehicle that appeared to have something dragging from it. As Filbert passed the vehicle, he noticed that the dragging item was a basset hound on a leash, "picking them up and putting them down as fast as he could."
>
> Filbert gave chase as the car turned eastbound on North 21st and finally stopped, but not before the poor dog reached the speed of 20–25 m.p.h. "and rolled several times."
>
> The car's occupants, a man and a woman, jumped out when Filbert told them they were dragging a dog. The couple became distressed and began calling, "Tattoo! Tattoo!"
>
> Tattoo, eight months old, appeared uninjured, but Filbert suggested the couple take him to an animal clinic to be checked out. No citation was issued.[1]

Both of us have had times in our lives when we were "picking them up and putting them down" as fast as we could and still getting nowhere. Sometimes our lives have felt like one long, continuous workday. And everyone we talk to seems to have the same complaint: "There just isn't enough time to fit in everything that has to be done." A "Dennis the Menace" cartoon expressed it well when it showed the boy straggling home and declaring to his mom, "It got dark before I was through with the day."

///////////// ♥ **Time Is Money** ♥ /////////////

The pace of the race in this, the last decade of the century, has caused Americans to cherish their time over any currency or product. The old adage "Time is money" has become truer than ever before in history. Time is a limited commodity—a resource we cannot manufacture. And as with any resource, its value has skyrocketed as its availability has diminished.

One expert in American demographic trends has even predicted that time will be "the new currency" of the coming decades:

> For several thousand years, mankind has used money as the primary means of establishing value. While money will continue to play a major role in our decisions and actions, by 2000 we will have shifted to using *time* as our dominant indicator of value.[2]

It's easy to see that this trend is already underway. Even during hard economic times, businesses that save us time and make life more convenient—such as mail order businesses—are prospering. In 1989, ninety-one million people made a shop-at-home purchase, and they cited convenience and time savings as their primary motivations for shopping by mail. The alternative means having to take precious time to find a parking place, walk to the store, hunt for the product, and perhaps stand in line to purchase it. No wonder people seem to prefer the convenience of a catalog and their telephone, even if they have to pay a little more.

Shopping isn't the only chore you can take care of by phone. You can now take care of most of your errands quickly and easily with just a phone call and a credit card. Banks, dry cleaners, and grocery stores are now providing courier and delivery service. Shipping services will come to your door to pick up packages for overnight delivery. And you can fax your order for pizza, Chinese food, or bagels.

In fact, mealtime is the site of some of the most dramatic changes in our "time is money" lifestyle. Less than a century ago, meal preparation took a big chunk out of every day. Then came convenience foods and fast food. And now, for some, gourmet takeout seems to be just the thing. These upscale, precooked meals have found a niche among the busy people living in modern suburbia.

Even if you prefer to cook at home, faster ways of preparing food have quickly taken over. Food industries experts estimate that 80 percent of U.S. households now have microwave ovens—and use them! In response to the burgeoning "TV dinner" market, Stouffers now offers eighty-six entrees that can be prepared in five minutes or less. Although some of these products and services are pricey, money is not the object. The primary criterion seems to be shaving minutes off the time it takes to put food on the table.

People have become so conscious of time being worth money that a man in Florida billed his ophthalmologist ninety dollars for keeping him waiting an hour.[3] The point of his argument was clear: In a society as demanding and fast-paced as ours, one cannot afford to waste time waiting.

There is no doubt about it, these are the days of the time famine. Most of us are careful not to waste a moment. As a result, many of us have learned to maximize our time by doing two things at once. In a recent Orange County California poll, 85 percent of those surveyed said that they often find themselves doing more than one thing at a time. That explains why you see women applying cosmetics and men shaving with their cordless razors while driving through traffic. And haven't all of us tried to stuff a hamburger in our mouth and balance a drink while pulling away from the fast-food drive-through?

Our obsession with efficiency is a mixed blessing. Sure, some of our time-saving inventions have been a godsend—who would want to go back to the days before disposable diapers, push-button phones, or automatic teller machines? But the other side of the coin is that the luxuries of time have all but disappeared from our lifestyle as well. The efficient (and impersonal) production line long ago replaced the skilled craftsperson laboring to produce a masterpiece. It seems a waste of time to do your own baking when you can so easily buy it at the store. The idea of traveling to Europe by sea rather than by air seems almost ludicrous.

The ironic thing about all of this is that our time-saving inventions have not given us more leisure time. In fact, they have only increased life's speed. A growing proportion of Americans say they always feel rushed. But what are we rushing toward? And what, in our hurry, are we leaving behind?

⁄⁄⁄⁄⁄⁄ ♥ Something Is Missing ♥ ⁄⁄⁄⁄⁄⁄

Psychologists from Sigmund Freud to Carl Rodgers have emphasized the primacy of relationships in human life. And long before Freud, wise men and women recognized that human beings are incomplete without significant relationships. But in all of our rushing, it's easy to overlook this essential factor—to let our relationships become casualties of the rat race.

The essential part that others play in our lives can be traced back to our human beginnings. One can read in the first chapters of Genesis that God created man and pronounced him good. But God realized something was missing. In order to be happy and fulfilled, this new person needed a companion. So God made a woman and later confirmed the importance of intimate human relationships by instituting marriage.

Ever since the beginning, then, people have had a basic need for a relationship with God and with other human beings. We were created to live in relationship with others.

But relationships need one vital element in order to grow... time. Diana Ross was right when she sang "You Can't Hurry Love." Time is to the human relationship what water is to plants—essential! And yet time is precisely what we run short of in our hurried lives.

Increasingly, relationships are floundering for lack of attention. According to national surveys, the average dad spends less than ten minutes a week in one-on-one communication with his children. The average married couple spends less than twenty minutes a week engaged in meaningful conversation. Most adults (especially males) have a difficult time identifying three intimate friends. Few people manage to invest much time in pursuing a relationship to God through personal study and prayer. We have, in a manner of speaking, become "too hurried to love."

In particular, our hurried society is changing family relationships. Most sociological experts agree that managing the average family of 2.4 kids is a full-time job for one of the parents. But for many families, living on a single income is simply not economically feasible. In the past decade, wages have stagnated, yet housing costs in most metropolitan areas have soared and the cost of living has skyrocketed. Most of us work extremely hard to make a living, but the cost of raising a family in today's economy makes us spend just as hard.

Consequently, there is seldom enough time to pay much attention to our need for family intimacy, rest, or recreation. Many of us tell ourselves that if we work hard now we'll have time for these things later on. But what most often happens is that the years go by and later never comes.

//////////// ♥ The Hurried Life ♥ ////////////

It ought to be clear that the hurried life just isn't good for us—and it could even kill us. Hurried people always appear to be rushing somewhere, but they're not really more productive or successful. Instead, they are driven, anxious, tired, and confused. And many suffer from high blood pressure, ulcers, depression, chronic allergies, and other stress-related illnesses. (Some psychologists use the term "hurry sickness" to refer to these stress-related syndromes.)

Hurried people are the ones who have said yes to so many things that now they seem to be on the verge of panic. Just observing their lives brings to mind the schoolyard rhyme: "When in trouble, when in doubt, run in circles, scream and shout."

And it's also clear that the hurried lifestyle rapes relationships. It substitutes a forced flurry of activities for the deep intimacy that is indicative of true friendship. And it makes you put off or cut out those relationship-building activities that are absolutely vital to your long-term happiness and well-being.

Do you ever find yourself "economizing" on your relationship efforts when you are hurried or tired? We call this practice "skimming." It's the relationship equivalent of putting on makeup in your car. It involves being physically present with people but not fully with them mentally. You're skimming when you come home to be with your family and your mind is still on your job. You're skimming when you're talking with a friend on the phone but trying to read, write, or type at the same time. You're skimming when you're not fully attentive to the person you're involved with.

It was a sobering experience for each of us when we realized that the frantic pace at which we lived was causing us to make skimming an everyday habit. Our relationships were on hold and our hurriedness was keeping us from experiencing the joy of really loving others. We each had to come to terms with the fact that although we claimed to value relationships above all else, we were really more concerned with the tasks we felt needed to be accomplished. Our focus was misplaced, and we were missing out on appreciating the little things that make life worth remembering.

That's what the hurried life can do to you.

And that's what we hope this book can prevent.

///////// ♥ It's Okay to Be Busy ♥ /////////

But at this point you may be protesting, "I *like* being busy! I like my days to be full and exciting. I'm not ready to slow down and retire from life."

Neither are we. We're busy, too, and we wouldn't want it any other way. But there's an important difference between being busy and being too hurried to love.

Erma Bombeck has made us laugh on many occasions. But sometimes she's more than funny; she's profound—as shown in a little piece she calls, "If I Had It All to Do Over Again":

> Someone asked me the other day if I had my life to live over would I change anything. My answer was no. Then I changed my mind. If I had my life to live

over again I would have talked less and listened more. Instead of wishing away nine months of pregnancy and complaining about the shadows over my feet, I'd of cherished every minute and realized that the wonder growing within me was to be my only chance in life to assist God with a miracle. I would never have insisted that the car windows be rolled up on a summers day because my hair had just been sprayed. I would have invited friends over for dinner even if the carpet was stained and the sofa faded. I would have eaten popcorn in the good living room. I would have worried less about the dirt when you lit the fireplace. I would have taken time to listen to my grandfather ramble about his youth. I would have burnt the pink candle sculptured like a rose before it melted while being stored. I would have sat cross-legged on the lawn with my kids and never worried about the grass stains. I would have cried and laughed alot less while watching television and alot more while watching life. I would have shared more of the responsibility carried by my husband which I took for granted. I would have eaten less cottage cheese and more ice cream. I would never have bought any thing just because it was practical. When my child kissed me impetuously I would never had said "later on, now go get washed up for dinner." There would have been more "I love you's," more "I'm sorry's," more "I'm listening's." But mostly given another shot at life, I would seize every minute of it, look at it and really try it on, live it, exhaust it, and never give back that minute until there was nothing left of it.[4]

These are the words of a woman who realized life was rushing by her and who had the resolve not to let the pace of the daily rat race steal her joy in living.

But notice that Erma never said she regretted being *busy* with her life. What she regretted were the times when she "skimmed"—when she allowed everyday pressures to make her too preoccupied, too hurried, to fully appreciate those things that brought joy to her life. In the end, she realizes, those things will be the ones that really matter to her.

Being busy is just the way life is in this century—and will be in the next. Even though we may dream of living life at a slower pace, we can't realistically slow down too much. The salesperson has to live with the quota. The performer must constantly rehearse to keep the "edge." The athlete must train every day. The pastor must prepare for another Sunday. The therapist will always have another anguished soul to listen to. It's next to impossible to accomplish anything significant without being busy.

And being busy is not really bad for us—*if* we can manage to be busy without being hurried. We know busy people who have a great sense of accomplishment and are living out their life direction according to their established priorities. They are focused people who have a mission to accomplish, yet who love life and seldom appear rushed or hurried.

A busy life can be an exciting life. As in river rafting, it's the fast movement that makes for the excitement. And it is not the speed, but the lack of decisive action and planning (including time for rest), that can lead to disaster. With the proper perspective and priorities, busy people can live exciting, profitable lives.

Chances are, your life is going to be busy...but it does not have to be hurried. We believe the answer to our frantic lifestyles and our slighted relationships lies not in our slowing down, but rather in properly ordering our lives around priorities that really matter. Fortunately, we have an example of that kind of life to follow—a model for living lives that are busy but not too hurried to love.

The Answer to a
///////////////////// ♥ **Hurried Life** ♥ /////////////////////

The more we study the life of Christ, the more we are impressed with how he managed his life. He knew he was on a mission from God, but he never let that mission drive him to the place where the task came before the people.

In spite of an incredibly demanding schedule, Jesus never became hurried. He paid attention to his own needs for solitude, rest, and relationships. He never apologized for taking the time to go off alone to a quiet place to pray to his Father God. He never allowed the success of his ministry to sidetrack him with diversions that would have taken energy and time away from his primary purpose and relationships.

Jesus never allowed the comments from those who misunderstood to stop him. He constantly found himself in situations where he was maligned, threatened, opposed by his "friends," misquoted, weakened physically, and severely tempted. Yet with a confident calmness, he stayed at his task and remained committed to his relationships.

Jesus never seemed to hurry anywhere, yet we are told that he finished every single one of his objectives during his short life. The night before his agony on the cross began and his earthly life ended, he looked toward heaven and prayed, "I have brought you glory on earth by completing the work you gave me to do" (John 17:4). And as he drew his last breath, he made the incredible statement, "It is finished" (John 19:30). Nothing essential was left undone.

We believe the key was his intentionally focused lifestyle. The kinds of complexities that tie most of us up in knots never seemed to concern Jesus. He kept his life focused by setting limits. He chose twelve (not twelve hundred) into whom he would pour his life for three years (he had an end date in mind). Rather than getting caught in the success trap that says bigger is better and that enough is never enough, he chose to own only those things he could easily carry with him as he walked among the people. His ability to set limits was the reason he could focus fully on the moment rather than fuss around with a million worrisome concerns.

Luke 10 tells a story from the life of Christ that gives us dramatic insight into his values and priorities. Jesus is visiting the home of two sisters, Mary and Martha. Martha was very concerned about making the proper dinner preparations for their guest. After a time, she became intensely upset with her sister, who would rather just sit at Jesus' feet and listen. In her flustered and hurried state, Martha gave Jesus a piece of advice: "Lord, don't you care that my sister has left me to do the work by myself? Tell her to help me!" (Luke 10:40). Jesus replied, "Martha, Martha...you are worried and upset about many things, but only one thing is needed. Mary has chosen what is better, and it will not be taken away from her."

Jesus' response indicates the value he placed on relationships. He was teaching Martha that time invested in meaningful conversation is just as important—if not more important—than "getting things done."

Most of us find ourselves sympathizing with Martha. The pressure we feel to please others by being what we think they need has caused us to continue adding nonessentials to our agendas. It sometimes seems as if we spend our lives living up to others' expectations. Add to that our own standards of what makes a person a success, and we end up only a hair's breadth away from being totally stressed-out. No wonder we're too hurried to love!

Purpose—Perspective—
/////////// ♥ **Process—Practice** ♥ ///////////

We've written this book to help busy people like you keep from becoming hurried people. Our purpose is to suggest some changes in your thinking and some practical changes in your lifestyle that will help you make time for the things that really matter in your life—especially your relationships with your family and your friends.

We're not writing to tell you to "slow down"—whether or not you need to slow your pace will depend on your individual circumstances. And we certainly aren't trying to convince you to change your basic personality. Instead, we hope to help you know who you are, to make sure of your life direction, and to structure a life that has room in it for relationships. That's the best antidote we know to the hurried lifestyle.

The changes we suggest center around "four Ps":

♥ *Purpose.* We've found that when our purpose gets fuzzy, our whole life becomes a blur. Establishing a life direction and setting clear, well-thought-out goals is a key factor to a fulfilling life. It is not so much the pace of our race that matters, but the assurance we are headed in the right direction. We begin, therefore, with showing you some practical ways to get your life in focus by discovering and clarifying your overall life purpose and your shorter-term goals.

♥ *Perspective.* How we view life affects the way we live it. That's why having the proper perspective about ourselves and our relationships can have such a profound effect on the way we live. Most of us cannot substantially change our environment, but we can change our perspective on how we view life and the world around us. In particular, if we are to have any hope of developing and maintaining meaningful relationships, we must dispel three damaging myths that are propagated by our culture. The second section of this book will help you examine and come to terms with those myths.

♥ *Process.* Socrates was famous for using profound questions to get clarity on the complex issues of life. And that practice still holds. Asking the right questions at the right time can enable you to get your hurried life under control and keep it under control. We believe you will find the profoundly simple process outlined in the third part of this book very helpful.

♥ *Practice.* This book was designed to be extremely practical. Its final chapters will be committed to applying the concepts that have been developed earlier to the four most important relationships of your life. We suggest dozens of proven ways to enhance your relationships with God, friends, spouse, and family.

So, how can you tell if this book is for you? How can you know whether you are just busy or too hurried to love? Maybe it's time you weighed in to see if you're exceeding your load limit. The Life Pace Inventory at the end of this chapter will help you get a feel for the amount of hurry in your life and what it might be doing to your relationships. It's a "hurry check-up" that just might help keep you from burnout and allow you to enjoy life without packing an unfair burden that squeezes the fun right out of your life and relationships. At any rate, it will help you find your starting point on the road to a more fun, more focused, less hurried life.

♥ Life Pace Inventory ♥

Circle the word(s) that best describes you. Be honest—this is for your personal growth.

	1	2	3	4
1. The past week my relationship with God has been…	poor	complacent	okay	growing and vital
2. I have worked out or been physically active ____ times in the past week.	zero	5 or more	1–2	3–4
3. In the past week I have spent ____ of focused time with my children. (Give yourself a 3 if this doesn't apply to you.)	less than 30 minutes	less than 60 minutes	more than an hour	more than 2 hours
4. In the past week, I have spent ____ of focused time with my spouse. (Give yourself a 3 if this doesn't apply to you.)	less than 90 minutes	less than 3 hours	less than 6 hours	more than 6 hours

	60 hours or more	59–50 hours	49–54 hours	45 hours or less
5. In the past week I have spent —— working.	60 hours or more	59–50 hours	49–54 hours	45 hours or less this week
6. The last time I went on a date alone with my spouse or a friend was…	cannot remember	last month	last week	this week
7. My friendships could be described as…	out of touch	numerous but shallow	satisfactory	growing and vital
8. My life overall is…	running on empty	maxed out	fast-paced but meaningful	productive and fulfilling

Using the numbers at the top of each column, add up your score. Below is a scale to help you interpret your score and determine if this book is for you.

29–32	Give this book to a friend—you don't need it!
26–28	A good score!—but keep reading.
17–25	Time to evaluate—you will probably find this book encouraging.
Below 16	This book is a must—don't put it down!

///////////////////////////////////// ♥ **ACTION STEPS** ♥ /////////////////////////////////////

1. As you looked at your score from the Life Pace Inventory, what did you learn about your lifestyle?

2. What areas of your life did you identify as needing the most attention?

3. In what areas do you think you are doing well?

4. If you were to boil life down to the core issues, what would you write down as those things that matter most to you?

5. Write down the names of the five-to-ten most significant people in your life. Keep these people in mind as you read through the rest of this book.

Part One:
PURPOSE

The Road That Goes Somewhere

// ♥

"This is the true joy in life, the being used for a purpose recognized by yourself as a mighty one."

—George Bernard Shaw

"The greatest thing in the world is not so much where we stand as in what direction we're moving."

—Oliver Wendell Holmes

During the Great Depression in Ireland, the government put unemployed peasants to work building roads. Delighted to have jobs again, these men worked energetically alongside each other, singing songs.

Then one day the peasants realized that the road they were building didn't go anywhere. It just rambled out into the countryside and stopped. The road had no purpose, except to give them something to do.

When that reality sank in, the songs stopped. The workers became listless and started grumbling among themselves. As writer George Moore, who recorded this story, observed, "The roads to nowhere are difficult to make. For a man to work and sing, there must be an end in view."

Many Americans today are like those Irish peasants. They have been building roads going nowhere. Now they are waking up and realizing how much they have given up and how little satisfaction it has brought them. Successful Baby Boomers are growing skeptical and disillusioned about their payoff for giving so much of their lives to the corporate chase. They look back on all of their toil to see a series of broken and empty relationships and missed opportunities. They are lonely, burned out, angry, and listless—like the Irish road builders, they have stopped singing.

For Karen Glance, it came down to all those little packets of shampoo. She remembers the morning she opened her bathroom cabinet in St. Paul and counted 150 that had followed her home from hotels in dozens of cities. In an interview with *Time* magazine, this former apparel executive stated:

> I was a workaholic, a crazed crazy woman. I was on the plane four times a week. I just wanted to get to the top. All of a sudden, I realized I was reaching that goal but I wasn't happy. A year would go by and I wouldn't know what had happened. It really came down to my saying, wait a minute. The value of life might not be in making my $100,000-plus yearly income.[1]

We have talked with people at all stages of life who realize their lives are in pieces—that they are moving in umpteen different directions but actually going nowhere. Unfortunately, many people live under the delusion that the answer to this hectic, hurried life is to slow the pace. In a *Time*/CNN poll, 69 percent of five hundred adults said they would like to "slow down and live a more relaxed life," in contrast to only 19 percent who wanted to "live a more exciting, faster paced life."

Much has been said and written in recent days about the benefits of what author Amy Saltzman calls "downshifting,"[2] changing to a slower pace. And many people, including several popular authors, seem convinced that the answer is a radical change of pace—moving out of the big city, for instance, or changing jobs. As already stated, we disagree. Much of the time, we believe, withdrawing from the rat race is neither realistic nor effective.

Obviously, there are times when downshifting is necessary—when life is simply going too fast. Chapter 6, in fact, outlines a process for reviewing your commitments and slowing your pace when you have taken on too much. But most of the time, being too hurried to love is *not* a consequence of being too busy. Instead, it results from being too busy *doing the wrong things*. The primary culprit is not a fast pace, but a lack of direction.

Without direction, people quickly come to resemble the balls in a pinball machine—bouncing around frantically, reacting to different situations and people, until they finally run out of energy and drop out of sight. Or they become like ships with a broken rudders—drifting (or, more often, speeding) aimlessly through life, at the mercy of changing currents and high winds. And more often than not, relationships are the principle casualties of such an approach.

But it doesn't have to happen. You don't have to bounce wildly or drift aimlessly through life. Instead, you can chart a course, hoist up the sails, and channel your efforts toward desired results. The joy of it all is that, with a course charted, you can then enjoy even a fast-paced life while keeping your relationships vital.

⁗ ♥ Going the Right Way ♥ ⁗

Whether you are too hurried to love is determined not by how fast you move, but by whether you are headed somewhere—and moving in the right direction. The pace of your life, in other words, is not the primary issue. Many people are busy all day long, but their busyness does not produce any significant results. The well-known management consultant Alec MacKenzie underlined this fact when he said, "Nothing is easier than being busy and nothing more difficult than being effective."[3]

It is better to do one or two meaningful tasks per day than to carry out a multitude of nondirected activities. Or, as the popular lecturer Zig Ziglar puts it, "There is no point in doing well that which you should not be doing at all."[4] We would add: there is no point in being busy with activities that don't take you where you want to go in life.

Imagine a good-looking young man in Los Angeles who climbs into his beautiful convertible with plans to go north to San Francisco. He is cruising along on a gorgeous, sunshiny day. The only trouble is that he is on the southbound freeway headed for San Diego! It makes no difference how comfortable that young man is or at what speed he is driving; he is not going to get to his desired destination. He would be better off riding a three-speed bicycle heading north.

During a transatlantic flight, an airline pilot announced to his passengers, "Folks, I've got some good news and some bad news. The bad news is that we're lost. The good news is that we've got a great tailwind!" Without a clear direction and a fix on your position, you'll never find your way to your destination. You may appear to be going along in life at a pretty good clip, but unless you know where you're going, all is for naught.

During my doctoral studies, I (Charlie) remember hearing Peter Drucker, the father of modern management theory, make an important distinction between being *effective* and being *efficient*. Effectiveness is doing right things. Efficiency is doing things right—in the most advantageous manner. Both are important, but effectiveness must come first.

If you are going on a trip, for instance, efficiency means that you consider the fastest, least expensive way to travel. But effectiveness means that you start out by identifying your final destination correctly. If you don't do that, efficiency will not make any positive difference in your trip. If you're only efficient, you may appear to be making tremendous progress, but really go nowhere. Even worse, you may end up far from where you wanted to go.

The *Los Angeles Times* recently carried a story about a California truck driver who asked a police officer in Duluth, Minnesota, for directions. His written delivery instructions told him to traverse Boggs Avenue, Independent Boulevard, and Meadow Brook Lane. The officer, who had never heard of those streets, suggested they look at the invoice. And it was then that the driver discovered he was thousands of miles off target. He was supposed to be in Duluth, *Georgia*. He had driven many long, hard, dusty miles in the wrong direction.

A few years ago, I (Charlie) worked on a project with a man who was extremely efficient. He refused to let anything fall through the cracks. He had a list for every task he ever attempted. People praised him and admired his productivity. As I got to know him, however, I saw that he had no close friends and was rapidly alienating himself from his wife and children. It was at that point that I personally realized that I can miss the mark in life if I focus on efficiency instead of effectiveness—if I spend too much time figuring how to get where I'm going and not enough time figuring where I want to go in the first place. That realization was confirmed by the sad confession of a wealthy businessman who told me, "I spent my whole life climbing the ladder of success, only to get to the top and find it was leaning against the wrong wall."

Making schedules and lists is important, and knowing how to make good use of your time is crucial to successful living. Working hard is also vital. But going in the right life direction is the too-frequently overlooked bottom line of effective living. It is the key to managing a life that is busy but meaningful—a life that is not too hurried to love.

Setting Out Your
//////////////// ♥ Grand Design ♥ ////////////////

How do you make sure you are going in the right direction? One of the most helpful things you can do is to take the time to formulate a specific statement of what you perceive your life direction to be.

In a sense, this life-direction statement represents your Grand Design in life. According to one dictionary, *design* means an "intended or desired result." You were created for a purpose—a desired result. A life-direction statement sets down your understanding of what you believe that purpose is—why you exist. It also comprises what you *want* your life to be all about—your desired result. In other words, it is the wall you want your ladder leaning against.

The apostle Paul, that great spokesman of the early Christian church, knew the importance of having such a life direction. He wrote, "I run straight to the goal with purpose in every step" (1 Cor. 9:26 TLB). And though this translation uses the word *goal*, what Paul was really describing was an overarching *life purpose*—his Grand Design.

That distinction is important because determining a life direction is different from what people usually think of as "setting goals." Goals comprise the "what" of your life; direction is the *"why"* of your existence. While goals have to do with specific achievements, direction is concerned with the motivation behind those achievements.

For example, if you said, "I want to make a million dollars before I am thirty and give 40 percent away to charity" you would have a goal. A life-direction statement, on the other hand, might be, "I want to use my resources in a spirit of philanthropic giving."

Note that the goal mentioned above is limited by external factors, but the life-direction statement is not. Whether or not you are able to make a million dollars and give away a certain percentage will depend partly on your circumstances. But you can always be generous with what you have, whether you are wealthy or poor. You can follow your life direction, in other words, regardless of circumstances.

When you determine a life direction, you choose your own way. You decide how you will live and what your priorities will be. Your life direction is your statement of what you will give to life, regardless of what life gives you. Once it is established, it will always be there to help you keep on course—serving as your rudder to allow you to navigate the rough sea of life.

When conducting "Life Focus" workshops around the country, I (Charlie) have spent time with many people who feel their lives are empty or that they have no control over what happens. Often they are waiting for the right person or opportunity to come along before they can really start living. They find it hard to make decisions concerning how they should spend their time. It has been my experience that once they determine their life direction, their life starts to change. A number of these people I have kept in touch with over the years have confessed this has been true for them.

What a Life Direction
//////////// ♥ Can Do for You ♥ ////////////

What, then, are the advantages of establishing a clear life direction and using it as a guide? Here is a summary of the benefits:

(1) *A life direction gives you a sense of satisfaction.* Author Gail Sheehy's book, *Pathfinders,* the sequel to her bestseller, *Passages,* provides dramatic contemporary testimony to the sense of satisfaction that a clear sense of life direction can bring. Sheehy defines a "pathfinder" as a person who has "already met a test," someone who successfully navigated through a crisis period and emerged better and stronger. Her book, in essence, is an attempt to isolate the factors that turn people into pathfinders.

In preparation for writing *Pathfinders,* Sheehy surveyed sixty thousand people between the ages of eighteen and eighty and personally interviewed several hundred individuals. The resulting data pointed to a particularly clear-cut conclusion: "The one constant in the lives of people who enjoy high well-being...was a devotion to some cause or purpose beyond themselves."[5] Interestingly, she adds: "Given the contemporary cultural tilt, 'purpose' is the one element you or I might not have predicted as crucial to life satisfaction. Yet the results were dramatic.... The distinction is so considerable that it makes the current pop philosophy of looking out for Number One sound like a national suicide pact."[6]

The apostle Paul knew firsthand the satisfaction that comes from following a clear life direction. He wrote: "I run straight to the goal with purpose in every step..." (1 Cor. 9:26 TLB). And although Paul's race was not always easy—he suffered beatings, imprisonment, shipwreck, physical ailments, and many other troubles—he was able to say, "I have learned the secret of being content in any and every situation, whether well-fed or hungry, whether living in plenty or in want (Phil. 4:12). And near the end of his ministry he wrote with satisfaction, "I have fought the good fight, I have finished the race, I have kept the faith" (2 Tim. 4:7).

(2) *A life direction gives you a sense of stability,* even during unstable times of your life. That was the experience of Viktor Frankl, a Jewish psychiatrist who survived the Nazi concentration camps. His remarkable book, *Man's Search for Meaning*, describes both the atrocities he and his fellow prisoners suffered and the deeper attitudes they held. And it attempts to answer a critical question: Why did some who were spared the crematorium survive, while others just gave up and died or even took their own lives? The survivors, he concluded, were those who had some sense of meaning in their lives, something to live for, some hope for the future. He writes, "Woe to him who saw no more sense in his life, no aim, no purpose, and therefore no point in carrying on. He was soon lost."[7]

What Frankl observed in the concentration camp was that people can put up with a lot of "what" in their lives if they know the "why." If you have a sense of life direction or purpose, in other words, you can lose everything else and still hold on to your reason for living.

The period in my life when I (Charlie) moved from seminary teaching to full-time consulting was one of tremendous change for me—in lifestyle, schedule, responsibilities, and even relationships. Although the transition had been my choice, on some days I struggled with my decision. It was during those days that I pulled out my life-direction statement and was assured that everything was all right. My simple, one-sentence life-direction statement gave me the perspective and sense of stability I needed to keep going.

(3) *A life direction helps you build better relationships.* A life purpose can have an important and positive effect on our relationships with others—which is what this book is all about. William H. Mikesell, minister, psychologist, and author of *The Power of High Purpose,* observed many years ago that

a tragic aspect of the minor-purpose individual is that he does not feel close to mankind. People are not close to him because he is not close to himself. Whether he wants to be or not to be, he is a little island unto himself. He also feels quite apart from God.[8]

You can expect the reverse to be true as well. When you solidify your purpose or direction in life, you secure your own place in the universe. You know why you exist, and thus you create a healthy environment for relationships to grow and develop. In addition, you will probably manage your time better and make space for relationships in your life.

(4) *A life direction helps you make wise choices* by putting decisions in context. Planning consultant Bobb Biehl likes to say that "nothing is meaningful without a context." That's why a life purpose can be so helpful when it comes to decision making. It puts the various options in perspective and thus allows us to choose even between difficult options—to distinguish good from better, appropriate from inappropriate. It enables us to see clearly which choices will get us where we want to go.

The importance of context was illustrated for me one day when I (Charlie) picked up my oldest daughter, Charlotte, from school. As she got into the car she told me happily, "I got a four on my Spanish test." Why did she feel so good about such a low grade? Because it wasn't really low at all. On the typical grading scale of a hundred, of course, a grade of five would of course represent a miserable failure. But in this case, five was the top grade possible. Taken in context, four was an excellent grade.

Since I have identified my life purpose, it has been the grid against which I have made many tough decisions over the years. A good example was my decision to give up officiating at high-school wrestling matches.

Having gone through college on a wrestling scholarship, in my postcollege years I became involved in officiating, and I did it "on the side" for many years. The pay was good, and I enjoyed the work, even on top of my regular duties. But as my consulting practice expanded and my two daughters grew, I faced a hard decision concerning this commitment of time. And I found my personal life-direction statement essential in making that decision.

My life-direction statement is this: *"I exist to love, serve, and glorify God by helping individuals and institutions to be focused and to maximize their God-given potential to impact their world for God."*

When I first started the officiating, I was teaching at a Christian university, so part of my reason for officiating was to get out into the world to share my faith and also to learn to be more assertive. These reasons clearly fit my life direction.

But circumstances changed when I quit my university job and began consulting. My new work presented me with many daily opportunities to share my faith. Assertiveness was no longer a problem for me. And I needed more time to help maximize the God-given potential of two very important people—my teenaged daughters.

When I looked at my decision in light of my life-direction statement, I could see clearly that the time I spent consulting, presenting Life Focus seminars, and parenting fulfilled my life direction better than officiating wrestling matches. So I gave up the officiating. This is just one of many occasions when my life-direction statement has helped me distinguish between the good and the best opportunities.

Discovering Your
///////////// ♥ **Purpose in Life** ♥ /////////////

Do you remember the incident in *Alice in Wonderland* in which Alice is talking to the Cheshire cat? Alice is a bit confused about her direction, so she asks the cat, "Would you tell me, please, which way ought I to go from here?"

"That depends a great deal on where you want to go," replies the Cheshire cat. "I don't much care where," says Alice, to which the feline replies, "Then it doesn't matter which way you go."

Most people, of course, really *do* care where they go. So do you. You want your life to have meaning, and you can see the benefits of having a focus, direction, and purpose in life. The difficult part is finding out what that purpose should be. There is no formula for mapping out purpose, no magic button to push to determine your life direction. Somebody else's purpose won't do for you.

So how do you go about establishing your unique purpose life direction? The first step is to realize that you already have one! Your life already has a purpose, given to you by God. Your task, then, is to discover what your life direction is, not to create one from scratch.

Victor Frankl says that people "detect rather than invent" their purpose in life.[9] We like that choice of words. Each person, we believe, has an internal monitor or sense that provides an awareness of his or her own uniqueness and the personal contributions he or she can make. In Frankl's words, "Everyone has his own specific vocation or mission in life.... Therein he cannot be replaced, nor can his life be repeated. Thus, everyone's task is as unique as is his specific opportunity to implement it."[10]

Your life direction may be deep inside you and slightly fuzzy at this point. But it can be drawn out, identified, polished, refined, and focused. And the best way to do that is to answer a few simple but profound questions:

(1) *What do you enjoy doing?* What activities bring you pleasure and satisfaction? What would you like to spend all of your time doing if you had the chance? Look hard at those activities, because they will probably give you a clue to your life direction.

Don't fall into the trap of believing that nothing you like can be good for you. When the psalmist said, "May [God] give you the desire of your heart" (Ps. 20:4), surely he was saying, in part, that God put those desires there in the first place. The desires of your heart—the things that bring you greatest joy—can provide important clues to what your life purpose should be.

Our Creator wants us to discover our special abilities and then invest them in the world. Writer Frederick Buechner states it this way: "The place God calls you to is the place where your deep gladness and the world's deep hunger meet."[11]

So where is your deep gladness? Do you love words? Numbers? Music? The out-of-doors? Working with people? Remember that God created you. He wants you to be who you are—to do what you love to do and are called to do. There is no greater satisfaction and joy than that of doing what you were meant to do. What you enjoy doing says so much about you and your potential for shaping the future. It is an important ingredient in determining your life direction.

(2) *What do friends say your strengths and talents are?* The wisdom of Solomon as recorded in the book of Proverbs often advises seeking the counsel of others. That's good advice

today as well. As you attempt to discover and clarify your life direction, it makes sense to turn to people you respect and ask them what they feel you do best.

It is important to look beyond the obvious for your gifts, and other people can help you do this. You may have an unusual ability or one that is so deeply a part of you that you can't see it in yourself. Maybe it's a quiet or nonflamboyant quality, such as the ability to listen. (A quality listener can be as effective in changing lives as a quality speaker.) The observations of a friend can help keep you from overlooking such quiet strengths.

Your special abilities are there, waiting to be acknowledged. Ask a friend to help you discover them. Your strengths and talents should be an integral part of your life direction.

(3) *What is your motivation?* Having worked with young, hard-driving entrepreneurs, humble country pastors, corporate executives, single parents, and many other types of people from various walks of life, we have concluded that all humankind can be divided into two motivational groups: those who are driven by greed, and those who are motivated by need. People are driven either by the desire to control, possess, and capture the things and people around them or by the desire to make a significant difference in their world by correcting or meeting the needs that concern and burden them.

Greed, of course, cannot be the key to a positive life direction. Centuries of human experience point to greed's ultimate futility—it can never be fully satisfied, and it never brings true fulfillment.

Your response to need, however, can provide you with valuable clues as to what your life direction should be. What stories especially interest you, draw you, or pull at your heart when you watch TV, read the newspaper, or walk around your block? It might be the plight of abandoned animals, the lack of effective school-board leadership, the shabbiness of the church property. Maybe you are keenly aware of the lonely latchkey child next door, the debris washed up on local beaches, a particularly dangerous intersection. Whatever the need that stirs you, pay attention. Your inner response to need can give you important insight into what your life direction should be.

The Old Testament gives us an excellent example of a man driven by need. Nehemiah was an educated man who held the trusted position of cupbearer for the Persian king Artaxerxes. He had a good life, but he was concerned when he heard about the broken wall surrounding Jerusalem, the capital of his homeland. Without walls, people of that day were totally helpless. Nehemiah records, "When I heard these things, I sat down and wept. For some days I mourned and fasted" (Neh. 1:4). More important, when Nehemiah heard of the broken walls of Jerusalem, he became motivated to do something about it. From a career standpoint, he was better off serving in the king's court, but he was motivated by need, not greed. Nehemiah traveled to Jerusalem, rallied the people, and restored the walls.

(4) *Where does God fit into the picture?* Your relationship with God is a foundational issue in choosing your direction. Do you believe in God? Is God an important part of your life? Do you believe in the validity of commands that God has given to us? Is God going to be at the heart of your life and purpose? Do you believe that God has provided a place for us to spend eternity with him? Answers to these questions will greatly influence your purpose and direction in life.

If you believe, for instance, that the best is yet to come in eternity, then you need to be careful about how you treat people now. This is not just a sanctity-of-life issue, but an eternal-life one. It involves the reality that every person who walks on planet earth embodies an eternal spirit which lives forever. No other created thing can make such a claim. Without a regular reminder that the human spirit is eternal, it's easy to be drawn into the snare of giving "things" priority over people. It should be clear, then, why your response to God and your view of eternity is so important in determining your life purpose and shaping your relationships.

(5) *What do you want on your tombstone?* "I told you I was sick" is often the humorous reply to the question of what one would like to have as their epitaph. But seriously, asking this question can be helpful in clarifying your life direction. In a sense, your desired epitaph is a direction statement, because it indicates your desired outcome for your life—the anticipated end result of your life direction. It can also help you see more clearly that your current path may not be taking you where you want to go.

A consulting client of mine (Charlie) was putting in long hours in an attempt to build his company into the nation's best. He had little time left to spend with his wife and children. And yet, when asked what he would want on his tombstone, the man quickly replied, "He was a loving husband, father, and friend."

I asked, "Are you sure it isn't 'He had the number-one office in the country'?" "No!" was his vehement reply. Then, being a bright man, my client quickly saw that his current behavior needed to change if his desired epitaph was to ring true.

⁄⁄⁄⁄⁄⁄⁄ ♥ Improving Your Aim ♥ ⁄⁄⁄⁄⁄⁄⁄

Henry David Thoreau once said, "In the long run [people] hit only what they aim at." What are you aiming for? What do you want people to say about you as your days come to an end? What, in other words, is your life purpose?

We believe it is tragic that so many people live and die without ever being aware of their life direction, their purpose. Everyone is living for something, but not everyone knows what that something is. And that lack of purpose is the reason so many are rudderless, stressed out—too hurried to love.

But again, it doesn't have to be that way. Your life already has a purpose. It is there, ready to guide you if you just make the effort to discover it, write it out, and follow it. But you can't just pull a purpose statement out of a hat. And you can't force or fake a life direction; you must find it as you look carefully at who you are and seek God's plan for the gifts and abilities he's given you. This may require some hard soul searching.

Will your life direction ever change? In our experience, adults who have understood the difference between goals and life purpose and have made the effort to understand what their life direction should be will be able to formulate a life-direction statement which in essence holds true for the rest of their lives. Minor adjustments may be necessary along the way. And specific career choices and goals may change quite a bit. (This happened with both of us.) When you first determine your life direction, you may even need to make a *U* turn. But once you take the time to choose carefully and begin moving down the right road, your life-direction statement will remain a dependable North Star to help you keep on course over a lifetime.

The specific wording of my (Dave) life-direction statement has changed several times over the past few years, and I am still in the process of making minor adjustments as I learn more about myself and discover more about God's plans for me. The essence of my life direction, however, has remained constant: *"I exist to love God with my passion and use my God-given gifts of teaching, listening, creativity, and leadership to encourage the people around me to do the same."* That written, established statement has helped me maneuver my way through several major changes in my life without straying completely off course. It has allowed me to remain both firm and flexible in my choices.

The Action Steps at the end of this chapter can assist you in the process of identifying your own life direction. Keep in mind as you work on them that embodied in your simple statement is a complexity of convictions and experiences that touch the deepest level of your being. What sounds merely nice or noble to one person may hold a great deal of meaning to you.

Don't be like the majority of people who spend more time planning a Christmas party or a vacation than they do determining their purpose in life. Take the time now to purposefully design your life by discovering your life direction and move toward more effective living and more meaningful relationships in our fast-paced world.

///////////////////////////////// ♥ **ACTION STEPS** ♥ /////////////////////////////////

1. Write out your answers to the following questions.

   a. What are the twelve things you enjoy doing the most?

   b. What are some of the hurts, problems, and needs you see in your world and would like to help solve?

   c. Do you want God to be at the center of your life and purpose? Why?

   d. What do you and your friends see as your ten greatest strengths or talents?

   e. What do you want printed on your tombstone?

2. Starting with the phrase, "I exist to…," write for five minutes without stopping. You can write multiple purpose statements or one long statement during that time; the important thing is to keep writing.

3. Go through what you have just written and underline what you think are the key words. Then narrow your choice down to the three most important—the three words that most accurately describe why you think you exist.

4. Using the material you have written and your three key words as a resource, write out a one-sentence life-direction statement. You might find the following examples helpful:

> I exist to serve others by using all of my talents and abilities and by helping others develop to their fullest potential.

> I exist to love God, family, and friends and to show this love by helping people see life with increasing clarity and cope with life's pressures and challenges.

> I exist to assist others in doing something that will make a significant change in the world and work for the betterment of people.

> I exist to affirm others in all they can become.

Part Two:
PERSPECTIVE

3

The Myth of Success

// ♥

"Most people don't know what they really want—but they're sure they haven't got it."

—Alfred E. Newman

"The greatest among you will be your servant."

—Matthew 23:11

On most days there's a voice in our heads—sometimes small, sometimes thundering—that says, "Be successful!" Maybe that is why we subscribe to a magazine called *Success*. And we're far from alone! The goal of material success is pounded into most Americans from a very early age by family, friends, and the media.

Parents urge their children to work hard so that they can become "somebody." Schools continue the pressure with competitive test scores and rewards for outstanding performance. Winning is the premier goal in athletic endeavors. Motivational speakers preach the gospel of visualizing success in order to achieve it or the philosophy of "dream it today—claim it tomorrow."

Society demands success. Bookstores overflow with volumes instructing people how to become successful, make more money, and accumulate power. And they suggest, either tacitly or openly, that these are the goals that should drive every red-blooded American. Magazine headlines boldly promise shortcuts to success. And all the media—television and movies as well as books and magazines—glamorize the rich and famous as models for the "successful" life. No wonder the voice inside us all screams out—"Go for it!"

Different cultural environments, of course, carry their own specific definition of success. For a minister, success may mean church growth, effective outreach, community prestige, denominational recognition. A woman in the corporate world may prize acceptance and recognition as much as financial security. In an immigrant community, the proprietor of a thriving family grocery store may carry the same aura of success that the CEO of a multimillion-dollar conglomerate carries in the world of high finance. And to a child in a ghetto, the drug dealer's fine clothes and a big car may represent the epitome of "making it."

The different aspects of success may not appeal equally or simultaneously to everyone. Some people initially become seduced to work for only one brand of success—recognition, for example, or influence. But over time, the drive for one kind of success tends to lead to the others, because our culture rolls all of these temptations into one collective model—the "good life" of wealth, power, and prestige.

///////// ♥ The Myth of Success ♥ /////////

The apparent advantages of success are so appealing that they are difficult to resist. Almost without thinking, most people tend to feed their ambitions and raise their pressure gauges to satisfy the demands of success and experience its rewards. But the fantasies of success presented in the world almost never incorporate the real-life consequences. Instead, the typical dream of success promises wonderful ends that seem to justify virtually any means.

More than a hundred years ago, Ralph Waldo Emerson recognized that the idea of success as the "sweet without the bitter" is nothing more than an illusion, and a tragic one at that. "I do not wish more external goods," he wrote, "neither possessions, nor honors, nor power, nor persons. The gain is apparent; the tax is certain." A century and a half later, Emerson's wisdom is still as valid as ever. But our dreams of success are, if anything, even more colorful and illusory.

As time passes and hard work starts to pay off, a person naturally feels a certain satisfaction in his or her accomplishments and tends to overlook the price that's been paid. But the price is real, as many who have climbed the success ladder have discovered. In the words of one very successful woman entrepreneur: "I had to ask myself the question: Is what I want inscribed on my tombstone really 'She was a heck of a businesswoman'?"

I (Charlie) remember feeling a tremendous sense of satisfaction as I crossed the stage to receive my Ph.D. degree. And I deserved to feel proud. Yet unknown to me at the time were the consequences of my success—my relationships had sustained tremendous losses during those years of concentrated study. Then, having finished my formal education, I found myself caught in a vicious "success trap"—even while devoting myself to a life of service at a private university. I wanted to produce more and to have more than those who were around me. I wanted to publish and speak. I wanted to get ahead in my field. And I did—but the damage to my relationships continued. Looking back on those years, I can see clearly that my hurried drive to obtain recognition and influence spilled over and harmed my relationship with God, family, and friends. It did more damage than any of my accomplishments could offset.

What I learned during those years—and later, as I tried to repair the damage—was that success can be very seductive, even habit forming. I also learned that the habit called success can be deadly to my love for people and life.

As a culture, we have been sold a lie. We have bought into a subtle, yet damaging myth: that our success can be measured by our possessions and our performance...and that we can be happy only if we achieve that kind of success.

The problem with this kind of thinking lies in what it does to a person's perspective. Defining success in terms of dollar signs and status symbols and encouraging that kind of success as a goal usually results in radical and damaging transformation of attitudes and motivations. Material things become objects of affection. People become commodities to be used. Playing becomes subordinate to winning. Absolute rules become relative guidelines. And individuals end up worshiping themselves.

And again, it's all a lie. The reality is that few people prevail with a success-at-any-cost ethic. And of those who do, even fewer genuinely enjoy the end results. When the popular idea of success is your goal, you can never be satisfied.

Gordon MacDonald, in his book *Ordering Your Private World*, comments that "success should never be pursued as a goal. If you make success your goal, you are setting yourself up for disappointment."[1] He is right. There are countless reasons why making success your driving goal is—at best—harmful to you and your relationships.

///♥ The Truth About Success ♥///

Because the myth of success is so pervasive and so deadly, you must challenge its place in your thinking if you want victory over the hurried life. A proper perspective on success is imperative to healthy living and fulfilling relationships. If you let your attitudes become infected with the common view that success is defined by what you gain and what you get, you will find it all too easy to become too hurried to love.

The best way to confront myths and false perceptions is with the truth. The following four truths about success will help dispel the myth and start you on the road toward a healthy alternative.

Truth #1: Success Is a Moving Target

Success, as the world understands it, is usually out of your control and just beyond your reach. Because it is determined by changing external standards, you may achieve it tomorrow, only to find it redefined the day after. What was considered a sign of success when you are young—a certain salary, a certain position, or a certain house in a particular neighborhood—may no longer carry that "successful" aura when you are older.

We recently heard a young married couple congratulating themselves because they managed to buy a house in the high-priced Southern California housing market. To them, the ability to buy a house at all spells amazing success. But as that couple grows older, they are likely to find that their standard of house success will change. They may well find themselves longing for a new and bigger house in a different location.

Yes, success is a moving target. And because the meaning of success is constantly shifting, achieving the goal of becoming successful is next to impossible.

Aristotle's deceptively simple statement that happiness is the result of "living well and doing well" illustrates just how vague and impersonal the notion of "success" is. Until you get a clear perspective on what "doing well" really means to you, your ambitions are liable to fluctuate aimlessly with your circumstances or become an addictive drive—an inner voice that screams, "Enough is never enough!" You may come to view success as health when you're ill, wealth when you're in debt, power when you're feeling downtrodden—in short, whatever you happen to be lacking at the moment. Success becomes a means of filling a void, of patching over your inadequacies, of covering up your failings. Instead of capitalizing on your assets and moving ahead—that is, instead of truly doing well—you allow your shortcomings to dictate your dreams. Success and frustration thus become inextricably linked.

Truth #2—Pushing for Success Zaps the Joy Out of Life

Many of my (Charlie) consulting clients see themselves as competitive, ambitious, success-driven professionals. They tell me they love their work. But then, in the same breath, many will admit that they never have time nor energy for the pursuits that give them any real personal joy. When I ask if their ambition for success brings them any happiness, many give a perplexed shrug.

A drive for success does generate a certain heat and fervor that, for many, feels like pleasure. But when this pleasure comes at the cost of personally meaningful activities, interests, and relationships, the net effect is almost invariably negative.

The drive for success takes the vital edge off life, especially when it crosses over into an addiction. Just like some drug dependencies, "successoholism" can at first seem to enhance performance but soon starts having disastrous results. Stories of superstars whose careers have been destroyed or put in jeopardy as the result of some substance addiction are all too common today. The results of an addictive drive for success are similarly destructive: burnout, exhaustion, disillusionment, and the loss of joy and meaning.

Even a more "normal," nonaddictive drive for success can be harmful. Studies have shown that in the competitive world of baseball, with its multimillion-dollar salaries, the motivation of pushing for success can actually damage performance. Rumors leading up to a trade often cause players to strive especially hard to boost their performance. But the records of fifty-nine players involved in midseason trades from 1964 to 1981 show that their batting averages dropped during the period preceding the trade. After the trade, when the players stopped trying so hard to succeed and just played the game, their batting performance rose by an average of thirty points, exceeding their previous averages.[2]

I (Charlie) remember once talking to a highly successful pastor in the Northwest. This man's church had doubled in size in only eighteen months. He was often asked to speak at conferences. Plans were underway to build a huge church facility. But the pastor was miserable. He told me his life was just not fun anymore. He found his joy diminished—not just over his ministry, but over life in general—even though he had taken some exciting trips and was blessed with a loving wife, loyal children, and even two beautiful grandchildren. He admitted to me that his drive for success had taken the sparkle out of his eyes and the zip out of his step.

Truth #3—The Drive for Success Pushes Us Out of Control

The drive for success is a leading contributor to the hurried lifestyle because it is so hard to bring under control.

One reason for this is that success is often linked to performance, which in turn is often tied to the ability to make money. It's easy to feel powerless when it comes to these two areas of life; even people with the finest priorities and the best intentions find themselves struggling. Money and performance are so closely linked to personal survival and self-esteem that many people live in fear of losing either one. As a result, falling under the control of these two driving forces is all too easy.

The drive to perform may be an adult version of the need to "be a good boy or girl" in order to be loved. Or it may be a reflection of a culture that seems to value people only for what they produce and to discard them when they are no longer productive. Regardless of where it comes from, the need to perform can easily become a driving force for many men and women. It can take many forms: perfectionism, workaholism, the inability to say no to requests—even, ironically, the drive to be a perfect parent. When it comes to money, the average family feels handcuffed to an attitude that has little regard for relationships. Anxiety hits them as they dress for work on Monday morning. It jumps out at them when they total their monthly bills and see that their checkbook balance in the checkbook isn't as big as the total of their bills. They are anxious either because they are struggling to get ahead or because they are groping to get by.

Like you, we want to take adequate care of our families. It's important to us to engage in "significant" work. We like to be able to dream a little and plan a lot. And there's nothing wrong with any of these things. But we must realize that we live in a culture that wants to program our dreams and manipulate our plans. The world in which we earn a living doesn't always share our convictions as husbands and fathers, and it has a bad habit of withholding rewards from people who are not driven to success and making money. Our world makes it difficult to keep the success drive under control.

Truth #4—Relationships Pay the Price of Success

If you are highly motivated by success, you may find that your working hours lengthen, your friendships suffer, your family life develops problems, and you develop physical complaints as the years pass. In short, you may endure a lot of hardships that cause you to feel like a martyr to your work.

Personal sacrifice is no guarantee of professional success, of course. At the same time, success as commonly defined in our culture is rarely achieved *without* such sacrifice.

Successful business men and women, if they are honest, confirm this fact. As advertising expert David Ogilvy observed in *Confessions of an Advertising Man:* "If you prefer to spend all your spare time growing roses or playing with your children, I like you better, but do not complain that you are not promoted fast enough."[3]

Tom Peters, who coauthored two of the most widely read books on the subject of work in the twentieth century, confirms this fact. His second book, *A Passion for Excellence,* sets forth the mandates for success—or excellence, as he terms it—in the work arena. And he draws his discussion to a conclusion by talking about the cost of success. An honest but alarming statement appears in the last page of the book:

> We are frequently asked if it is possible to "have it all"—a full and satisfying personal life and a full and satisfying, hard-working professional one. Our answer is: NO. The price of excellence is time, energy, attention, and focus, at the very same time that energy, attention and focus could have gone toward enjoying your daughter's soccer game. Excellence is a high cost item.[4]

This is the assessment of an expert: Success often comes at a high price. And the experience of many supports his statement. Divorce, angry kids, and failing health are not usually spelled out as the *requirements* for success, but they are too often the *result*.

Company presidents may talk about the importance of the family. They may say they are committed to their employees' marriages and kids. But the actual posture of the top brass is usually seen on promotion day, awards day, or payday.

An executive who doesn't want to work overtime on Saturday because his or her son has a Little League game is made to feel guilty—and is unlikely to be the first choice for a promotion. A salesman who passes up a transfer because the move would be too demanding on his or her family is considered unambitious—and, more likely than not, doesn't get another chance. A woman who steps off the career ladder for a few years to stay at home with her children will have a hard time getting back on the ladder again—even on the bottom rung. Like it or not, success in the marketplace is often achieved at the expense of success in relationships. The system is set up that way.

The Alternative
//////////////////////// ♥ to Success ♥ ////////////////////////

The drive for success as our culture defines it is ultimately futile and unfulfilling. But what's the alternative? Surely it's not any healthier to drop out of all activity and quit trying to achieve anything! Rabbi Harold Kushner, author of the best-selling book, *When Bad Things Happen to Good People*, points to a healthier alternative:

> Our souls are not hungry for fame, comfort, wealth, or power. Those rewards create almost as many

problems as they solve. Our souls are hungry for meaning, for the sense that we have figured out how to live so that our lives matter, so that the world will be at least a little bit different for our having passed through it.[5]

This simple but profound statement contains the answer to the success trap. Rabbi Kushner is talking about the distinction between driving for *success* and striving for *significance*.

What's the difference? First, the drive for success is usually "I" centered. It involves what "I" want or what others tell me "I" *should* want. It sounds like: "Look what I have done!" The focus is on "me" and what "I" have accomplished.

The desire for significance, on the other hand, is usually "other" centered. The focus is on the impact and influence I can have on other people and on the world around me. It can sound like: "I have really made a difference. People have been helped. Conditions have improved." A sense of personal significance arises out of self-respect, pride, conviction, purpose, and the love of family and friends.

Erich Fromm, one of the great thinkers of our time, put it very aptly: "The essential difference between the unhappy, neurotic type of person and him of great joy is the difference between get and give."[6] That seems to be the bottom-line distinction. Success wants to see how much it can get. Significance wants to see how much it can give. The famous humanitarian Albert Schweitzer caught the essence of this when he said, "Of this I am certain. The only ones among you who will be truly happy are those who have sought and found how to serve."[7]

Success is signaled by the acquisition of wealth, power, prestige, or fame. Success is often determined, therefore, by outsiders—colleagues, family, the public, or the media. Significance, on the other hand, points you in the direction that is signaled by a sense of quiet confidence and personal fulfillment, which reflect the values you have chosen.

Whether you are oriented toward success or toward significance can make a big difference in how you approach life and work. Because a success orientation provides an external rationale, it tends to encourage competition. It is often accompanied by dissatisfaction, anxiety, and material desire. Therefore, if you are driven primarily by the desire for success, you may have a surplus of ambition that prevents you from taking pleasure in the process or in your achievement or in your work as an end in itself. What matters most is the reward—the praise, the money, the power, or the recognition your efforts earn. This can quickly tip the scales from being appropriately busy to being too hurried to love.

If you have strong significance motivation, on the other hand, you may so love your work that you don't care whether others deem you a success. Because you appreciate the value of your accomplishments, you don't depend on external praise or rewards. And because you're not driven by the need for external reinforcement, you are less likely to become preoccupied with competition. You may strive to find a personal challenge and interest even in tasks that do not seem particularly interesting or likely to advance you. You may indeed put in very long hours and push yourself to do the best job possible.

At the same time, if you have a significance orientation, you will value personal fulfillment and other people. That means you will make room in your life for intimacy and relaxation. You will work hard, but you won't be a workaholic. And you may be led to make difficult decisions and even sacrifice material success in the interest of better relationships and other values.

Marsha Bristow Bostick of Columbus, Ohio, for instance, chose to give up a lucrative job in order to devote more time to her family. Marsha, then thirty-seven, remembers noticing with alarm that her three-year-old daughter, Betsy, had memorized dozens of TV commercials. That helped inspire her to quit her $150,000-a-year job as a marketing executive. She and her husband, Brent, a bank officer, decided that Betsy and their infant son, Andrew, needed more parental attention if they were going to develop the right sort of values.

Marsha explains, "I found myself wondering, How wealthy do we need to be? I don't care if I have a great car, or if people are impressed with what I'm doing for a living. We have everything we need."[8] She was working from an orientation of significance, not success.

The following chart summarizes the distinctions between success and significance:

Success	Vs.	Significance
"I" focused		"other" focused
external motivation		internal motivation
material orientation		people orientation
moving target		stable target
greed centered		need centered
present rewards		timeless achievement
one generational		multigenerational

What It Takes to
////////// ♥ Feel Significance ♥ //////////

Innate in every person is the desire to be significant. But few of us have any real understanding of what significance really takes. That's why so many people make the ultimately futile and frustrating climb to success.

Carol,[9] who has risen to be the editor-in-chief of a major publishing house, earns nearly a quarter million dollars a year. By most people's standards, Carol is successful, but at this point in her life she would not agree. For many years, she found her quest for professional recognition and material gain exhilarating. But the sacrifices Carol made to get to the top and the quality of her life outside work have left her feeling empty and disillusioned.

Gwen has also made it to the top of her profession, but she has a different perspective. She has a positive sense of direction that encompasses her whole life, not just her professional career or her bankbook. Co-workers sense her genuine concern for them and can name many occasions on which she has made personal sacrifices to help them. Gwen's accomplishments have given her a true sense of significance.

Significance is not achieved by pushing to attain career stardom. Significance comes from focusing on others and using your God-given gifts and skills to make your world in some way a better place. And that's what we all need as human beings—not to be successful, but to be significant.

It's important to remember that we can be significant without being outwardly successful—or without really knowing just how much difference we make in the world. It's our motivation, our attitude toward what we are doing—not the visible result—that makes the difference.

We can learn a great deal about significance from an ordinary man named Kimball who led one his students to a belief in Jesus Christ. The student happened to be an impressionable teenager named Dwight L. Moody. Years later, the great preacher Moody spoke in a little chapel in the British Isles, where he showed a struggling pastor what it meant to be brokenhearted about sin. That pastor was F.B. Meyers. Meyers later inspired a young preacher whose name was J. Wilbur Chapman to turn his evangelistic crusade ministry over to a lowly YMCA clerk by the name of Billy Sunday. One evening a lanky sixteen-year-old boy sat spellbound under the preaching of the white-haired Sunday, and that night he trusted Christ for salvation. You may have heard of the boy. His name is Billy Graham.

The whole chain of events started with an "ordinary" man named Kimball who had no outward appearance of success, but who displayed a significance orientation. He focused on what really mattered, and as a result he played an important part in history. The label success does not have to be on one's forehead for one's life to be significant.

Significance
//////////////// ♥ **Comes First** ♥ ////////////////

Most of us unwittingly adjust our natural inclinations to fit the "success driven" mainstream. In doing so, unfortunately, we may sacrifice what matters most to us. The young doctor who loves research is persuaded to go into private practice. She quickly becomes accustomed to the high income but finds her daily routine unfulfilling and dull. The artist who earns a modest income through selling a few paintings and taking on an occasional commercial assignment becomes convinced by his family that he will never be respectable unless he gets a "real" job. He ends up with slightly more money and a desk job he finds boring.

It's easy to make choices like these in the name of success, only to find that the detours you've taken are neither productive nor satisfying. Learning to block out the external pressures and discover what truly motivates you is an essential first step toward finding your own track—one that leads to a feeling of significance and healthier relationships.

If you want to avoid being too hurried to love, you must recognize the falsehoods in the myth of success and at the same time grab hold of the truth that significance is the greater human need. Doing so will allow you room to be fully human—to be as good as you can, but not necessarily better than the next person. People who work hard and think of others can accept their shortcomings and inevitable failures because success for them is an by-product, not a goal.

It is motivation, not achievement, that makes the difference. And it is the motivation of significance that will lead you toward a healthy life.

Challenging the standard assumptions about success does not necessarily mean abandoning the goals that are usually associated with success. We all can benefit from a certain amount of praise and recognition. We all want to feel that we have some influence over the others in our lives. And we all enjoy the comforts that money can buy. But we must keep in mind that it is quite possible to achieve all these goals and still feel insignificant—like a failure. Although they may contribute to our well-being, they are not essential. Success can be important. But significance must come first.

///// ♥ Significance *Is* Success ♥ /////

A success orientation rarely leads directly to significance. More often, it creates an obstruction of guilt, anxiety, and pressure which must be overcome before one can have healthy relationships. A significance orientation, however, creates the ideal conditions for success to follow, and it frequently does, along with meaningful relationships.

When we talk about "having it all," we really mean living well and doing well: having the outer reward of external success and the personal feeling of significance. Attaining either of these goals is not easy, and sustaining a balance between the two can be even more difficult. To do it, you need to start with significance and make that your priority. Significance often leads to success, while success often fails to lead to significance.

One of the great patriarchs of the Jewish people, Moses, is a prime example of how significance can lead to success. He turned his back on the education, wealth, and power of Egypt. He was the adopted grandson of the ruler of the land. Yet, as his eyes turned from his own luxurious surroundings to focus on the terrible plight of his own people, the Israelites, who were living in slavery, he started on an unbelievable journey of great significance. This journey took him out of the comfortable Egyptian palaces to lead the hard life of a nomad. According to the success standards of Egypt he was a failure. But his focus was not on success, but on his people. Moses eventually led the Jewish nation out of slavery to their promised land. What Moses did from the very beginning had significance, no matter what the result. By the end of his life, however, he was not only significant, but also successful.

You might even say, then, that "significance *is* success." Significance means knowing that your values line up with those things that are really important to God. It means working to make a difference in someone's life. It means being free to use your work as a vehicle to facilitate your family rather than a force to hold them hostage.

We challenge you to be wise enough and courageous enough to disagree with the world's perspective on success. You might take some criticism, and you might not advance as quickly. But instead, you will maintain balance, peace, and healthy relationships. Putting your energy and focus into living a life of significance instead of being driven toward the elusive dream called success will help you take a major step away from being too hurried to love.

1. Write a paragraph describing the time in life when you felt most significant.

2. Who is the most successful person you know personally? Who would you say is the most significant? Why?

3. List the five things you have done that made you feel most significant.

4. List instances in which you felt pushed toward success. What has been the result?

5. How would your life change if your focus was on significance rather than success? What would you need to do to make that a reality? Write out one specific action step you could take this week to move in that direction.

The Myth of Being the Best

// ♥

"If I am what I have and if what I have is lost, who then am I?"

—Erich Fromm

"When you aim for perfection, you discover it's a moving target."

—George Fisher

The realization came slowly to me, but when it finally hit I found it very disturbing. I (Charlie) was becoming obsessed not only with being successful, but with being the *best*.

It started when I was offered the position of Chairman for the Christian Education Department at Talbot Theological Seminary. I had just turned thirty, and I was convinced I had arrived. In my mind, the Talbot C.E. department was the apex of Christian education. It had the most students and largest faculty of any nondenominational C.E. department in the country.

People suddenly started treating me differently when I assumed my new position. At professional conferences, I was in demand. I never lacked for friends or lunch invitations. Students started telling me how good I was as a teacher, and colleagues heaped affirmation on me for being in such a position at such a young age. I began to believe I could really be successful, even nationally known, like people I had admired all my life. And so I set the goal of being the best teacher at the seminary.

Not long after that, my relationships with my colleagues and my family began to change. I found myself becoming jealous of other teachers and manipulating circumstances in order to position myself professionally. I was putting in long hours, which kept me away from my wife and daughters, and I was enjoying my work less.

It was then I discovered that I was working under a myth that was not only restricting me, but slowly destroying my relationship with those important to me. The myth was: *You have to be the best!*

What does it mean to be the best? *Best* means being number one... being top dog. It means no one is better than you are. And best is what the world screams out for us to be.

Sports are a notable example. Football teams, baseball teams, hockey teams—participants in every kind of sport—go to battle every weekend to determine who is the best. Even as we write, a debate is raging in the media over which college football team is going to be awarded the mythical "National Championship." This winter the sports page was full of reports about baseball players receiving multimillion-dollar contracts from team owners trying to have the best team. And every four years the attention of the world focuses on the Olympics, where young athletes from around the world contend for highest honors in their sport.

But the "quest to be best" is not just limited to sports. Authors intently peruse the bestseller lists to see whose book came out on top. Television networks vie for highest ratings, salespeople strive for top sales, countries go head-to-head in competition for trade. Children on playgrounds still play out endless variations of "king of the hill," and their parents encourage that "competitive spirit." Even the parents of very tiny children want their babies to be the first to walk, talk, and sprout teeth.

Yes, people from all walks of life and with various passions spend million of dollars each year trying to be number one in some area. Some even become obsessed with it—often with tragic results.

You might ask, "But what is wrong with wanting to be the best?" It's a natural question. The media have convinced us that being best is what we all should be striving for. Many would even say that the struggle to be on top is healthy. But that struggle has a destructive side we need to be aware of if we hope to improve the quality of our life and relationships. Let's look at some sobering truths about being best.

Truth #1—Only One Can Be the Best

It sounds obvious, but it's easily overlooked: Only one person can be the best. Being the best naturally precludes anyone else. This means we can easily become jealous of others' success and progress. Relationships naturally suffer.

I (Charlie) found this to be true for me during the time when I was trying to be the best teacher at my seminary. When a student would mention to me that another teacher was really outstanding, I would smile politely and say, "Great!" But in my heart, I was saying, "Oh, *no* ..." If another teacher was good, that meant I might not be the best.

Deep suspicion and hostility often lurk beneath the superficial camaraderie of people involved in specialized pursuits. Why? Because everyone has his or her eye on the goal of being the best. This is not always obvious when you are starting out. But as you ascend the pyramid of your chosen specialty and the ranks begin to shrink, it's hard to avoid comparing notes on your colleagues' progress. There is a choice between cooperation and competition, even at this stage, but taking a cooperative approach may challenge the entire system of advancement.

Many professions routinely pit top performers against one another, forcing them to compete for high positions. It is quite possible, therefore, to be the best and end up without a friend. And if you don't reach the top, the alienation of the climb may leave you feeling defeated and burned out.

The "being best syndrome" that has become endemic to our American culture is also partly to blame for our general timidity and lack of initiative in accepting challenging goals. In the crush for top grades, for example, good college students routinely seek out the courses that guarantee them As, rather than taking the courses that might best engage their minds or equip them for the future. And career-ladder climbers routinely spend enormous amounts of energy jockeying for position and "covering their tails"—energy that could otherwise be applied toward development of a better product or better service.

In many ways, our society has become shackled by a "number one" mentality—the assumption that only the person on top is worthy of recognition. Do you realize the futility of this mind-set? In any given situation, there can be only one number one. And if being number one is the only worthwhile goal, that means anything less is subpar—even a failure.

Say, for instance, that the winner's time in a mile race is 04:32, and the next guy finishes in 04:33. Does that make the runner-up a failure? Of course not. But that is how he is often made to feel.

And there is some degree of truth to the assumption that to be second best is to fail. Can you list, for example, the *losing* candidate in the last five United States presidential elections? Many people can't, and even fewer can remember the runners-up in the five elections before that. Typically, we remember who won—who came out as the best. But we don't remember who came out second best; we even call him or her the loser.

Our world makes it clear that the successful man or woman must not accept second best. Successful people cannot put ceilings on their ambition and drive. In fact, the fastest way to end up in last place is to admit that you're satisfied with second place. With all this pressure to be at the top, it's no wonder that the average American family has credit cards at their limits, a mortgage they can't afford, both spouses working, and no time to keep in touch with one another. This approach to our accomplishments cannot help but have an ill effect on our self-esteem and our relationships.

Truth #2: Being Best Is a Nebulous, Fleeting, and Elusive Goal

The second truth about being best is that being best, like being successful, is a moving target; it is usually nebulous, subjective, fleeting, and elusive. How can a person know if he or she is the best teacher...the best consultant...the best pastor? It is often impossible to determine. So most of us find ourselves continually striving to be a little better. And still the elusive carrot called "best" keeps moving.

Even in situations where one *can* clearly be named the best—the champion of the World Series, for example, or the valedictorian of a college class—the distinction is often fleeting. Usually, it extends for only a year, as in the World Series. Sometimes, as with a track record, it may last for only a week or a day. The distinction of being best typically lasts only the time it takes for someone else to be better.

The elusiveness of being best can cause you to feel rushed or hurried—and eventually exhausted. Have you ever had the experience of trying to catch a mouse in your house? It is a frustrating experience. The little beast just darts back and forth, with no apparent pattern or reason. All the running around can quickly wear you out. And the pursuit of the best can have the same effect.

The fact that being best is fleeting and nebulous also means that achieving what you thought was the pinnacle can still leave you empty and disappointed. King Solomon, known throughout history as the wisest of men, hints at this sad reality in the first chapter of the book of Ecclesiastes:

> All is vanity. What does man gain by all the toil at which he toils under the sun? A generation goes, and a generation comes, but the earth remains for ever....All things are full of weariness; a man cannot utter it; the eye is not satisfied with seeing, nor the ear filled with hearing. (Eccles. 1:2–8 RSVB)

The word *vanity* in the original language gives an impression of a beautiful bubble that pops when it is touched and leaves us with nothing but empty hands. This can be a perfect description of what the drive to be the best can come to. Even if you do manage to reach the top, chances are that you will end up dissatisfied.

Truth #3: It Takes Extra Energy to Be the Best

No one would disagree that being the best takes extra dedication and effort. In fact, most books and speakers on the subject of getting ahead warn that you have to give "110 percent." The question is: Is it worth it?

Too much energy spent obsessing on being number one at anything will take away from our relationships and will throw us off-balance. To even try to be the best, we have to have a single focus, which tends to make us one-dimensional and to undermine our stability.

Our society's emphasis on the best, therefore, tends to create narrow, one-sided lives and to shortchange relationships. And this begins very early in life. Instead of being encouraged to try out many activities, for instance, teenagers are encouraged to specialize, to restrict their involvement to one or two extracurricular activities.

I (Charlie) once heard a high-school track coach badgering a young girl to drop out of band so that she could focus on her track event. He enticed her with hopes of a track scholarship. In essence, he was telling her that she could only be the best by giving her all to track—and that it was highly important to be the best. I believe he was doing her a grave disservice.

This is not to say that you should have no ambition or goals. Viewed within the broad context of your life, ambition can be a strong motivator, and goals can help you organize your time and energy. The danger arises when you allow just *one* goal to define your life and when that goal is the narrow and elusive one of being better than everybody else. While many people derive great pleasure from their accomplishments in a specialized field, nobody can rely on those accomplishments alone to provide complete fulfillment. By extension, this means that you may never be fully satisfied with your position, your awards, your kudos, your reputation if you've sacrificed everything else to achieve these things.

You need a certain amount of diversity in your life to feel like a complete human being. You need to take as much pride and joy in your accomplishments at home and at play as you do in, say, your job performance or your blue ribbons. You need to recognize that what you think, feel, and desire are as much a part of who you are as the title below your signature or the trophies on your wall.

There is abundant evidence that a narrow focus may be counterproductive in terms of accomplishment as well as happiness. One of the most influential of the many studies on this subject is the Grant Study of Adult Development at Harvard University, which chose 268 men from Harvard's classes of 1939 through 1944 and tracked their lives and careers for more than fifty years. The results of the study are telling. Those graduates who had the most successful careers were not necessarily academic superstars in school, and their professional ambitions have not wholly defined their lives in the years since. Instead, they allowed themselves to build strong, stable marriages and deep friendships. They made room in their lives for exercise, relaxation, and multiple interests and activities. And they have become bestselling authors, cabinet members, scholars, physicians, judges, and captains of industry. In short, they have kept variety in their lives rather than driving blindly to be the best.

This distinction is important, because variety tends to enliven our lives and to open us up to new ideas and opportunities. The ambition to be number one, on the other hand, tends to restrict us. Dr. George Vaillant, director of the ongoing Grant Study, explains: "There's no question that conventional lives statistically are the happiest. Stopping smoking, exercising, working hard, eating breakfast, and not getting divorced—all these humdrum things correlate directly with happiness."[1] If you invest a lion's share of your effort in one direction instead of cultivating a "conventional" and balanced life, you may end up losing all the way around.

▥▥ ♥ What Is the Alternative ♥ ▥▥

If being the best is an exclusive, elusive, and ultimately dissatisfying goal, what is a better alternative? We believe the answer lies in another distinction—the distinction between being *the* best and being *your* best.

I ran across a postcard at an airport that puts it well: "I may not be perfect, but parts of me are excellent." So does the well-known Army recruiting slogan: "Be all that you can be."

As previously stated, only one person can be *the* best. But every person alive can live a life of excellence. All men and women can do their personal best—working to develop their "excellent parts," striving to be all that they can be. And living with that motivation rather than the compulsion to be the best can free them to take risks, to attempt great things, to live balanced and healthy lives. People who are striving to be *their* best rather than *the* best are a lot less likely to be too hurried to love.

So forget the best—be the best you can be. The following chart summarizes the distinction between being *the* best and being *your* best.

Being *the* Best	Vs.	Being *Your* Best
is limited to one person		is available to everyone
demands a single focus		allows a multiple focus
has a short life span		encompasses a lifetime
is a product or end result		is a process

A plus to discovering the distinction between being *the* best and doing *your* best is that it allows for a more balanced life. Philosopher Bertrand Russell described such a life when he wrote that the secret of happiness is to "let your interests be as wide as possible and let your reactions to the things and persons that interest you be as far as possible friendly rather than hostile."[2]

This does not mean that you become apathetic and lazy in your approach to life. There is nothing wrong with wanting to be good at something. In fact, the desire to excel—to do your best—is an innate, God-given part of human nature. Wanting to do your best is admirable and healthy. But when you cross over the line into wanting to be *the* best, your need to excel can become an obsession that damages your well-being and starves your relationships.

We all need to pick the areas in our lives that are important to us and then simply strive to be our very best in those areas—stretching, risking, hoping, enduring. That's part of the process of the peak performance lifestyle. But ultimately, we are the only ones who can measure the quality of our own excellence. "If a man is called to be a street sweeper," Martin Luther King, Jr., once said, "he should sweep streets even as Michelangelo painted, or as Beethoven composed music or as Shakespeare wrote poetry. He should sweep streets so that all the hosts of heaven and earth will pause to say, 'Here lived a great street sweeper who did his job well.'"

That's worthwhile advice in our "king of the hill" society. Whatever your interests and priorities, the more you concentrate on living well rather than being the best, the more fulfilling your life will be.

/// ♥ **ACTION STEPS** ♥ ///

1. Can you think of a person or situation close to you in which the drive to be the best was destructive? What happened?

2. Think of someone you know who has the right perspective on doing his or her best versus being the best. Take that person out for coffee or a meal and an interview. Try to find out how that person developed his or her perspective.

3. If you do feel you're trying to be best, in what area are you making that endeavor? List what you are sacrificing in order to be best. Then ask yourself: Is it really worth it?

4. Do you need to correct your thinking concerning being the best? If so, what difference will a change in motivation make in your life? What action step can you take in the next week to change your thinking?

5. Write out on a 3 x 5 card or in your personal notebook: "I want to do my best, but I do not have to be the best." Put the card or notebook somewhere where you will see it every day. Read the reminder at least three time a day for the next month.

The Myth of Doing It All

/// ♥

"The trouble oftentimes with religious people is that they try to be more spiritual than God Himself."

—Frederick Buechner

"Men must be decided on what they will not do, and then they are able to act with vigor in what they ought to do."

—The Chinese philosopher Mencius

Many a heroic World-Series-winning catch was made against the side of my house in the desert during my Little League days. Many a last-second, tie-breaking shot was completed in my backyard when I (Charlie) was a teenager. And they were all done by me—in my imagination.

Even as child, I dreamed of being the President of the United States. I thought I could be anything. Anything was possible. The sky was the limit.

It is wonderful, even necessary, to dream. Dreams can motivate us, inspire us, energize us. They can keep us going during hard times. They help us reach beyond ourselves. Perhaps that is one reason we are encouraged to dream, even as adults. We are told to shoot for the top. We are told that the only limits are the ones we put on ourselves. We are told we can be and do anything we set our minds to.

But that kind of advice can also get us in trouble, as this poem humorously hints:

Bionic or Bust

Bionic's my name.
Achieving's my fame;
I juggle 10 balls
Without any strain.
Ball 1 is the office,
Where I'm an exec.;
Ball 2 is my home,
Where I keep things in check.
Ball 3 is the children,
Ball 4 is my spouse;
Ball 5 is den mother
For eight little scouts.
Ball 6 is the church
and committees I lead,
Ball 7's the refugees
I help to feed.
Ball 8 is my hobby
of painting still life;
Ball 9 is my parties
that everyone likes.
Ball 10 is the rest of
the things that I do—
I bake, sew, and garden,
To name just a few.

There's nothing beyond me,
I'm really quite able;
And if you've not guessed it...
I'm also a fable!
—Sybil Stanton[1]

If you are honest about yourself, you'll relate to the point of the poem: *Doing it all is simply a myth.* Given your particular physical, intellectual, and emotional makeup, certain paths are open to you and others will inevitably disappoint you. Even though you were created in the image of God, your humanity dictates that you have limitations. And you must recognize and accept those limitations if you ever hope to get control of your life and to maintain meaningful relationships.

My wife, Suzi, and I (Charlie) were planning our vacation one summer. After some discussion, we finally agreed on our destination; New England won out over Alaska. With that difficult decision made, we enthusiastically began to make plans. And almost immediately we bumped into our limitations. I had only three weeks of vacation. We could not visit every charming country inn in Maine, New Hampshire, and Vermont—and we could not afford some of them. We could not explore every hiking trail or travel every highway. We had to make choices.

The same is true of our daily lives. We must recognize our limits of time, energy, and resources. Then—sometimes with joy, sometimes with pain, and always taking our limits into account—we must decide what we are going to do. The average person can do ten, fifteen, maybe twenty things well. But the more activities we try to include in our lives, the more our energy will be diffused. When we spread ourselves too thin, we have less energy to expend on the important things in our lives. That's one way we become too hurried to love.

A Model for Living
//////////// ♥ **Within Limits** ♥ ////////////

When Jesus came to earth as the incarnate Son of God, he set aside certain of his divine rights. For a time, in order to identify with us fully, he accepted our human limitations— including the limitation of time. And what he did with those limitations can tell us a lot about how we can best deal with ours.

Jesus had a very busy life. His was a full schedule—preaching to the crowds, healing the sick, exorcising demons, responding to questions from friends and foes, walking from town to town. In fact, his many activities left him little time to be alone or to spend with just his disciples.

One insight we can gain into Jesus' personal organization of time is that he understood his own limits. We find Jesus often saying, "I must move on," "I can't stay," and "I will not do that." We also see that he *made* time for prayer and renewal, for relating to the people who really needed him, and for being with friends. He coped with his time limitations effectively by staying focused on his purpose and refusing to let others spread him too thin.

Jesus' whole life revolved around accomplishing his God-given purpose, yet he had time for some special friendships because he made right choices based on his life purpose and his understanding of what he could accomplish on any given day. That's why he was able to accomplish so much without seeming to hurry.

The commandments of Jesus also provide us with some helpful clues about how we can live effectively within our limits. Jesus never tells us we should not have a full schedule. He never suggests we should pull out of our fast-paced life to live quiet and restful lives. In fact, he tells us to get out in the world—to be salt and light. But he also makes it clear that we should remain constantly aware of our purpose and our priorities in order to make the best use of our limited time and resources. We will live most effectively by remaining constantly aware of who we are and what we can do.

Learning What to
///////////////////////// ♥ **Leave Out** ♥ /////////////////////////

Again, busyness is not the problem. The problem is we have too many opportunities, too many choices. The solution, therefore, lies in recognizing our limitations and making the right choices. And many of those choices will involve choosing what *not* to include in our lives.

A story is told of an entrepreneur who launched a new enterprise and hired a leading commercial artist to design a logo for his firm. When he received the completed artwork, he was very pleased. It was just what he wanted—plain and to the point. As he admired it, the bill fell out, and his jaw dropped when he saw the amount. So he called the artist and asked, "Why is the price so high when the design is so simple?" The artist answered, "The price is for knowing what to leave out."

Most of us could use some lessons in the fine art of leaving things out of our lives. It's a real struggle for most people, partly because we have been sold one of the most damaging myths in America today—that we can do or have anything we want if we just want it badly enough.

You've heard the spiel. You, too, can become a millionaire, run a corporation, fly to the moon, or become President if you really want to. It's been around for a long time. And now there seems to be a conspiracy of sorts—dominated by the advertising industry, politicians, and New Age practitioners—to support this illusion because it supports their sales pitches. The idea is: You can be anything you want to be ... *if* you wear the right cologne, vote for the right candidate, or follow the right guru.

But tempting as it is to believe that we can command our own destinies, we must face the fact that we simply can't do everything—no one can. (It's one thing, of course, to "know" we can't do it all—and quite another thing to live as though we believed it.) Each of us possesses a unique blend of strengths and weaknesses, opportunities, and limitations, many of which cannot be altered by using the right product, having the right attitude, or changing our environment. And if we don't pay attention to our limitations, we may find we're in over our heads with activities, commitments, and responsibilities.

Judith Viorst is one of our favorite authors. In her book *How Did I Get to Be 40 and Other Atrocities,* she includes a poem called "Self Improvement Program," a litany of activities in which she has participated—needlepoint, guitar lessons, advanced Chinese cooking, primal-scream therapy, and a half dozen other pursuits. Then she sighs as she concludes:

> And I'm working all day and I'm
> working all night to be good looking,
> healthy,
> and wise
> and adored
> and contented
> and brave
> and well read
> and a marvelous hostess
> fantastic in bed, and bilingual,
> athletic ... artistic ...
>
> Won't somebody please stop me?[2]

You, like Judith Viorst, may need to be stopped. If you haven't recognized your limits, you may just keep trying to do more. If you do, you can quickly get into what we call "option overload."

Option overload happens in your life when you have too many good things from which to choose. During the course of most days, you are offered many opportunities in which to invest your time. Each of these opportunities grabs your attention. Each one looks fun, or profitable, or worthwhile. If you do not come to terms with the fact that your time and our energy are limited, you can spend your days in a whirl of activity, yet have little to show for it. You easily cross over the line and become too hurried to love.

No—
//////// ♥ The Positive Negative ♥ ////////

There is, as usual, a simple answer to this dilemma—but it's not easy. It involves learning to say that two-letter word, *no*. Your time, in the hands of others, is governed by the "sponge effect"—the bigger the sponge you throw out, the more you'll be expected to soak up. So it's easy to become too hurried to love simply because you can't pronounce that two-letter word at the appropriate time.

You must learn to say no so you can say yes. If you refuse to say no to some of the good things that come your way, you may be unable to say yes to better opportunities when they arise. You may find yourself without the energy to do a good job at anything. If you cannot say no, you may find yourself losing out in the very areas that are most important to you.

Saying no takes practice. It's even a good idea repeat that word over and over again every morning, so that it will flow more freely from your lips during the day. For years we have gotten many chuckles from a list entitled "Easy Ways to Say 'NO'!" You might enjoy the list and even use some of the lines.

I'd Really Love To, But...

I have to floss my cat.
The last time I went, I never came back.
I've got a Friends of Rutabaga meeting.
None of my socks match.
I'm getting my overalls overhauled.
I'm attending the opening of my garage door.
I'm trying to see how long I can go without saying
　yes.
The man on television told me to stay tuned in.
My patent is pending.
I don't want to leave my comfort zone.
It's too close to the turn of the century.
I am going to count the bristles on my toothbrush.
My favorite commercial is on TV.

But why is saying no so difficult? Even with the use of humor and early morning practice, it is still hard, at times impossible, to pronounce that simple word.

Chances are, you want to do your fair share in life. You want to contribute positively to society and to your family. You want to be a "nice guy" and to "do a good job." And you don't want to miss out on any opportunities. Saying no becomes difficult when, because of timidity or misplaced altruism, you accept responsibilities that put you into option overload. When you do, you end up being unfair to your family, your friends, and yourself.

Keeping Your Eggs
///////////// ♥ **in One Basket** ♥ /////////////

When it comes to the difficult matter of saying no and leaving things out of our lives, we find it helpful to view life as a huge basket that is full to the top with fresh eggs. Each one of those eggs represents a relationship, an activity, or a responsibility. Any time we add a new relationship, activity, or responsibility, we are adding an egg to the basket, and an existing egg needs to be removed to make room for it. If this is not done, one of the eggs is going to roll out and break. And if we haven't made a conscious decision about what has to go, the egg that breaks may be one of great value to us—say, a vital relationship.

This egg-basket analogy helps keep us in touch with the reality that our "egg baskets" can only hold so much. We have our limits. As busy people with full "baskets," we must learn to manage our eggs carefully and responsibly. Whenever we're tempted to get involved in another project, we need to subtract one that we're currently working on. We must learn what to leave out of our lives in order not leave a trail of broken eggs behind us.

Accepting the fact that you have limits is not negative thinking. It is not fatalistic thinking, nor does it promote apathy. Accepting your limitations does not mean you have to live in poverty or that you cannot improve your lot in life. And it certainly does not mean that you cannot set goals or look ahead. Goals are important. You just need to make sure your goals are realistic and limited in number.

I (Charlie) remember attending my first time-management seminar as a young college professor. We were encouraged to set goals and map out what we wanted to accomplish. By the end of the day, I had set seventy-eight goals to accomplish over the next three months. I left that seminar feeling fantastic. And it was not until the next morning that reality hit me. I wanted to do everything on my list, but it was impossible! Stress set in. I became irritable. My relationships suffered.

What I failed to realize was that by not accepting my limitations I was setting up myself for failure. Since then, when setting goals, I have learned to ask myself three questions:

- ♥ Who am I?

- ♥ What do I want to become?

- ♥ What are the most important things that need to be accomplished in order for me to become the person I want to be?

Then I consider my full egg basket and decide what I will stop doing in order to make room for this new project.

Effective goal-setting, in other words, is more than just dreaming up goals and objectives. It also involves recognizing your limits and making plans to work within them. Keeping an eye on your "basket" can help you do just that.

Knowing Yourself Makes
//////////////////////// ♥ It Easier ♥ ////////////////////////

If you are ever going to accept your limits and learn to say no, it is vital that you have a proper understanding of yourself. Knowing who you are gives you a context for when to say no and when to say yes.

Let us illustrate with a parable. It's about a group of animals who decided to start their own school. The animals thought they should expand their abilities, so their curriculum included swimming, running, climbing, and flying.

The duck, a superb swimmer, was deficient in other areas, so he put all his energy into learning to climb, run, and fly, much to the detriment of his swimming. Since the rabbit excelled at running, he was advised to attend other classes, and he soon lost much of his famed speed. The squirrel, who was an $A+$ climber, dropped to a C because his instructors devoted their time to trying to teach him to swim and fly. And the eagle was severely disciplined for soaring to great heights instead of learning how to climb.

Obviously no one succeeded in this school. Everyone failed, because they were not allowed to take into consideration who they were.

For you to be able to make right choices—to say no when necessary and yes when appropriate—you must know and be yourself. Your decisions must be based on who you are—on your purposes and your strengths, not on those of your best friend or next-door neighbor. Going against your grain depletes your energy and wastes your time because you end up expending efforts in the wrong places. That is why you must persist in remaining true to yourself even if some people misunderstand and others try to fit you into their mold. Trying to do more than is appropriate for your abilities or your circumstances is a sign of weakness, not willingness.

Successful life management depends on a sensible assessment of how you operate and what you can handle. Part of the "too hurried to love" problem stems from the common tendency to ignore inner promptings and try to be something you're not. Let us suggest two important ways you should know yourself in order to make wise decisions and know what activities and commitments are appropriate in your life:

(1) *Respect your natural pace.* Dr. Hans Selye, the father of stress research, held that we all have a natural pace. Some people can be likened to racehorses—fast and vigorous—

while others are more like turtles—slow, but steady. Dr. Selye warned against violating either bent. If the turtle is pushed to run like a racehorse, it will either give up or die; if a racehorse is compelled to run no faster than a turtle, it will become frustrated and rebel. You need to find your own best stress level, the highest level of activity that is workable and pleasant.[3]

Again, the real issue is not the pace itself, but the pace which is best for you. Don't buy the idea that faster is necessarily better. If you are a turtle, make yourself comfortable with that pace and let it work for you. Remember that it was the tenacious tortoise, not the erratic rabbit, that won the race. On the other hand, slower is not the best if you are a racehorse. You want to run. You were created to run. And you do nobody a favor by attempting to crawl along at a steady turtle's pace.

Even if you are a racehorse, however, don't confuse racing with rushing. A champion thoroughbred covers a lot of ground, but always at a determined gallop, not jerking to the right or left or hurrying back and forth.

Many fast-moving individuals are more like roadrunners than racehorses. If you have never lived in the Southwest, you may not realize that roadrunners don't exist only in cartoons. Roadrunners are indeed swift, but they are also spasmodic. They never seem to know where they are going—or why. They're a poor model for anyone who wants to move ahead effectively.

The two categories we have described are, of course, simplistic. Many people may find they fit neither category. For example, we both thrive on the pace of a racehorse, but neither of us have the endurance of one. In order to avoid burnout, we have tried to slow our pace to economize our energy, but felt frustrated. Now we allow for our swifter nature, but also allow for more rest periods.

You cannot measure your ideal pace as simply as you can check the speed of your automobile. But in time you can learn where you operate most comfortably and productively and stay in that range. An authority on jogging says "If you jog too slowly, it may take forever to get the desired effect; if you jog fast, you just wear yourself out and get nowhere"[4] The same thing applies to life. Whether you are a racehorse, a turtle, or a combination, don't fight your natural pace. Discover it. Accept it. Go with it. Stick with the speed that gives you the best "mileage," regardless of what works for others. Your life will be much more productive—and more enjoyable—if you do.

Adjusting your pace is often easier if you keep your overall life direction in mind. Your overall purpose gives you a long-term perspective that can keep you from either rushing around aimlessly or simply plodding along.

Once, while on an extensive journey, Salvation Army founder William Booth received a letter from his wife urging him to pace himself for the long haul, not the short term. Her gentle warning is one many of us would do well to heed:

> Your Tuesday's note arrived safe, and I was rejoiced to hear of the continued prosperity of the work, though sorry you were so worn out; I feel the effect of all this excitement and exertion upon your health, and though I would not hinder your usefulness, I would caution you against an injudicious prodigality of your strength. Remember a long life of steady, consistent, holy labour will produce twice as much fruit as one shortened and destroyed by spasmodic and extravagant exertions; be careful and sparing of your strength when and where exertion is unnecessary.[5]

Ted Engstrom, former president of World Vision, also gives good advice at this point when he makes the observation that most people greatly overestimate what they can accomplish in a year and greatly underestimate what they can accomplish in five years. In the struggle to be less hurried, it's necessary to keep the big picture in mind. You need to realize that we cannot do it all in a year, but that with steady planning and wise choices you can accomplish a lot in five years—and beyond.

(2) *Know your capacity.* If you ran a circus, how many rings would you operate? One? Two? Three? How many are you operating now?

Your capacity is closely tied to your limits. A person can do only so much at one time. Everyone has a different-sized egg basket. Some situations are difficult because certain responsibilities are unavoidable. Many tasks, however, are self-imposed. Letting go of the hurried life may mean you must take a hard and honest look at what you have brought on yourself and ask whether you have exceeded your capacity.

Sometimes letting go of an involvement seems harder than hanging on. You may stay overcommitted just because you don't know how to give up a commitment. We have often observed, in our own lives and the lives of others, that the straw which finally breaks the camel's back—be it a job, a committee, or a project—often is not really necessary and does not serve one's overall purpose.

It's hard to admit poor commitment choices and then act to change the situation. I (Charlie) know, because I've been there. There have been times when I felt that my very reputation and self-respect were at stake. People counted on me. I couldn't let anyone down.

Then a friend told me, "Charlie, people only expect of you what you give. Keep giving, and they'll keep right on expecting. Stop being so available, and they'll stop expecting."

My friend was right. And so was psychologist M. Scott Peck when he wrote, "To be free people, we must assume total responsibility for ourselves, but in doing so, must possess the capacity to reject responsibility that is not truly ours."[6]

Letting Yourself
////////////////////////// ♥ **Be Human** ♥ //////////////////////////

When you put it all together—your natural pace and your capacity—what do you have? Superman? Wonder Woman? Probably not, because you are only human.

Does that disappoint you? It should be a relief. After all, your body and your friends have known it all along. When you are true to yourself, you follow your natural bent and encourage others to follow theirs. You don't compare yourself to others or impose your preferences on anyone. You were not made in a mold, so you shouldn't force yourself or others to conform to one. Life is much more enjoyable and less hurried when ducks are ducks and squirrels are squirrels...and people are people.

I appreciate the words which C.S. Lewis wrote to an American lady about the importance of accepting our limits:

> Don't be too easily convinced that God really wants you to do all sorts of work you needn't do. Each must do his duty in that state of life to which God has called him. Remember that a belief in the virtues of doing for doings's sake is characteristically feminine, characteristically American, and characteristically modern: so that three veils may divide

you from the correct view! There can be intemperance in work just as in drink. What feels like zeal may be only fidgets or even the flattering on one's self-importance....By doing what "one's station and its duties" does not demand, one can make oneself less fit for the duties it does demand and so commit some injustice. Just you give Mary a little chance as well as Martha.[7]

But how do you go about giving "Mary a little chance" in your life, especially if you're already in over your head? If you don't have any breathing space—we like to call it "wobble room"—in your life, take the time to size up your situation. What activities burden you most? Which ones bring you the most fulfillment? What can go?

When doing this evaluation, it's important to consider your life as a whole. You may be tempted to lean too far in the direction of being "practical" or "unselfish" and end up eliminating the activities that really bring you joy. Remember that recreation and relaxation are *necessities,* not extras. And then concentrate on identifying those activities and commitments in your life that have been imposed by others, that just don't fit your life plan, and that bring your life no joy and meaning.

Once you decide what activities can go, then you must determine how to go about removing them from your schedule. Unless the commitment is a minor one, you probably can't just back out of it with a phone call. Treat a major change as you would a new project and lay out your plan. Planning is as important to subtracting a priority as it is to adding one. (Chapter 6 gives some specific suggestions for backing out of an unwanted responsibility.)

As we saw in the previous chapter, having a life direction is the cornerstone for winning the battle against hurry, but it is not the only consideration. You will probably find that many positive opportunities come your way which do fit into your life direction, but which you need to refuse simply because your life is too full.

Recently I (Charlie) was asked to serve on the advisory council of a new ministry. What this ministry is trying to do fits my life purpose perfectly. Helping people accomplish their potential is what I am all about, but I needed to say no at this time because I had reached my capacity.

Managing your life so that you are not too hurried to love may well involve saying no to good opportunities that fit your life direction but would overload your schedule. Recognize your limitations, examine your motivation, determine your pace and capacity... and then practice in front of your mirror each morning saying, "No! No! No!" And as you do so, remind yourself that you are really saying yes to healthy living.

// ♥ **ACTION STEPS** ♥ //

1. How can a person determine if he or she is overcommitted? Write down a list of five or six "symptoms."

2. Why do you think it is so difficult for us to accept our limitations? Can you think of some instances when we should *not* accept our limitations?

3. Write out what you understand about your personal pace. Are you a turtle or a racehorse? Is there another animal that better represents your personal pace?

4. On a large piece of paper, list your *twelve* major responsibilities. Based on who you are and where you want to go (life direction), identify the *nine* most important and number them according to priority.

5. Write the three "extra" responsibilities (numbers ten, eleven, and twelve from the above list) on a separate sheet

of paper. Consider: If you chose to cut these three responsibilities from your life in order to give yourself more time
and freedom, how would you go about doing so? Outline a
preliminary plan for each. Then read the next chapter
before proceeding with your plan.

Part Three:
PROCESS

6

Keeping on Course

/// ♥

"The trick is not to rid your stomach of butterflies, but to make them fly in formation."

—Source Unknown

"I don't know the key to success, but the sure way to failure is to try to please everyone."

—Bill Cosby

Less than two seasons after Art Shell became the head coach of the National Football League's Los Angeles Raiders, he had led the team back into a championship game. For Shell, a former Hall of Fame tackle who had also paid his dues as an assistant coach, that victorious season was the fruition of twenty-two years of preparation.

Shell is tough, smart, commanding. His hold over his players is something to see. Some coaches punch out chalkboards to get their points across. Shell commands with soft tones and hard looks. His physical presence—he's 6 feet, 5 inches and 285 pounds—is enough to keep a team in check. When things don't go his way, he has threatened more than once to put his helmet back on and explain things more clearly.

But that's not the unique thing about Art Shell. Other

coaches are tough. Other coaches produce winning teams. But few other coaches share Art Shell's balanced attitude about what it takes to get the job done.

Art Shell is unique in that he prefers to finish his work for the day and then go home. "You don't have to stay here all night to get it done," he says. "You really don't. I want my coaches to go home and sit with their families, see their kids at night before they go to bed. I think it's important that your wife sees you before she goes to bed. It doesn't always work that way, but I think it is important. It creates a wholesome atmosphere for everyone involved."[1]

If a person like Art Shell, in a profession that is known for early burnout as well as for coaches sleeping in their offices during game weeks, can keep his life in balance and avoid being too hurried to love, then there is hope for all of us. And it all comes from keeping track of where you are in life.

Knowing Where
///////////////////////// ♥ You Are ♥ /////////////////////////

Bill Bradley, a former basketball great with the New York Knickerbockers and now a United States Senator from New Jersey, says, "To play good basketball, you have to have a sense of where you are on the court."

Bernie May, missionary pilot and executive director of Wycliffe Bible Translators, agrees. He feels the same is true with flying an airplane—especially under conditions that require the use of instruments.

It's called "positional awareness"—that sense of knowing where you are. On the basketball court, it can mean the difference between winning and losing. In flying, it can spell the difference between success and disaster. And in life, positional awareness can determine the difference between leading a productive, meaningful, enjoyable life and being too hurried to love.

In basketball, losing your positional awareness can lose you points—or even a game. That happened to the Georgetown University team in the early 1980s, during an NCAA National Championship game against North Carolina. In the final seconds of the fiercely contested game, Georgetown was a few points behind, but they had the ball. It was thrown into play, and the crowd roared as the Georgetown player who caught it prepared to make the play that could win them the game. Then, disoriented, he made his pass—directly to James Worthy of North Carolina (now with the Los Angeles Lakers). Time ran out, and Georgetown had lost, all because one of their players lost track of where he was.

In aviation, the consequences of losing positional awareness can be even more deadly. You can be a thousand feet above the ground and feel safe. But if your nose is pointed straight down or headed toward a fifteen-hundred-foot antenna, your time on earth may be cut short.

In life, losing your positional awareness can cause you to forget your purpose and make the wrong decisions. It's a leading cause of being too hurried to love. And you never know when it might happen. Life is unpredictable. And that means that even if you are trying to be true to your life *purpose,* even if you have the proper *perspective* about success, being the best, and accepting limits, you can still fall into option overload. You will still go through seasons of your life when your pressure gauge pushes toward the explosion point. There will be times, despite your best efforts, when you find that your relationships are suffering, your energy is depleted—you really have gotten off course.

So how do you keep track of where you are in life? Basketball players rely on their training, talent, and experience to keep them aware of their position. Airplanes have instrument panels to help pilots keep their bearings. And in order to keep your life on course, you need a *process* to help you stay aware of where you are and where you going. Such a process can act like the instrument panel in an airplane to give you positional awareness.

Just as in an airplane or on the basketball court, positional awareness in life is determined by the observation of your surroundings and by asking the right questions. Following are six questions you can ask to help keep yourself on course. Asked and answered in sequential order, these questions outline a process for examining your life, making wise decisions, slowing down if necessary, and keeping yourself on course.

Question #1: Have I Exceeded My Limits?

This is a question to ask yourself whenever you find yourself feeling hurried or flustered. If you are not sure how to answer it, you might ask a few of your significant friends to give you some honest feedback, or you might go back to our test in the first chapter.

If you do find that you are in over your head, admit it. Tell yourself, "I have exceeded my limits and need to do something about it." Then proceed to get your pressure gauge down by taking off some of the stress.

You may find that you do need to jettison some activities or responsibilities, and the questions to come will help you decide which ones must go. You may have to reduce superficial obligations on all sides and integrate personally important relationships and pursuits with professional goals. You may need to plan more social events that include your family and friends—and curtail other kinds of socializing. You may need to forget about decorating the nursery and spend that time playing with your newborn. Or you may need simply to give yourself permission to follow your instincts—for instance, to spend time with your son when he needs you instead of when your schedule permits.

In short, living within your limits usually means identifying and weeding out those goals, duties, and activities that do not fulfill your life purpose or that support the myths of success, being the best, or unlimited opportunity. The next five questions will help you determine what those goals, duties, and activities are.

Question #2: What Is Essential (Not Just Important) in My Life?

I have often heard that the good is the enemy of the best. That is true because good things always seems *important*. It's not that hard to sort out the bad activities. But it's often very difficult to distinguish good, important activities from those that are *best* for us.

When we sit down with people to help them figure out their life direction, we have learned not to ask them what their important activities are. If we ask them that, they end up listing everything they do! Most people think that what they are doing is important—otherwise, they would not be doing it. We have found over the years that if we alter the question slightly and ask them what is *essential,* the list gets shorter.

Our dictionary defines *essential* as "necessary to make a thing what it is—indispensable." The essential activities and responsibilities in your life are those activities that—

♥ few others could do,

♥ will create major, long-term negative consequences if left undone, and

> ♥ have multiple positive consequences if accomplished.

These are the activities that must take priority in your life, even if other important activities must go.

Jesus Christ gave us insight into the process of distinguishing the important from the essential when he stated:

> Do not store up for yourselves treasures on earth, where moth and rust destroy, and where thieves break in and steal. But store up for yourselves treasures in heaven, where moth and rust do not destroy, and where thieves do not break in and steal. For where your treasure is, there your heart will be also. (Matt. 6:19–21)

Jesus was saying, in other words, that the things which are truly essential in life—the places where we should "store up...treasure"—are the things that have *eternal* significance.

Those of us who work outside the home most likely spend a great deal of time in the business world—a world that has its own set of rules, values, and rewards. The ultimate reward, as we have seen, is success, defined in terms of more money, a loftier title, a bigger office, more prestige, more influence.

Unfortunately, as many people have discovered, any of those rewards can disappear in an instant. The company can falter or the management can "clean house," and our job can disappear overnight. An illness or physical disability can strike at any time and put an end to a promising career. As much as we strive for control over our lives, as much as we try to create security for ourselves and our family, we have to realize that it can all go away in a second. Control is simply an illusion; no one but God really has control over anything in this life. Any rewards we gain here on earth are just temporary.

The writer of Proverbs puts it another way: "Do not wear yourself out to get rich.... Have the wisdom to show restraint. Cast but a glance at riches, and they are gone, for they will surely sprout wings and fly off to the sky like an eagle" (23:4,5).

That doesn't mean we can't enjoy the rewards of our hard work—both the material rewards and the intangible rewards of challenge and accomplishment. After all, God gives us the ability to obtain them. But it does mean we should keep our *primary* focus on those activities and responsibilities that have significance beyond the tangible, the material, and the comfortable. There are lasting values that are different from those set by the world, media, or society. (Most of them involve our spiritual growth and the health of our relationships with other people.) The activities that further these values are the ones that have eternal significance, that help us "store up...treasures in heaven." They are the ones that are truly essential.

This does not mean *everything* you do has to be essential. When my (Charlie) daughter Jana became a cheerleader, for example, I chose to accept the position of vice president of the Pepster Booster Club. And I'd have to admit that being involved with the pep club is not essential, although it is related to some essential activities in my life. I accepted the responsibility of this time-consuming office because the activity of this club directly affects my daughter's well-being. My being directly involved in this club communicates to her that what she does as a cheerleader is important to me. In this sense, it is *related* to one of my essential tasks—that of being a good father. But if I reached the point that my duties with the Booster Club were making me too busy for, say, listening to

Jana when she needed me, I would have to cut back on this important but nonessential activity.

Keeping our priorities straight is the issue here—and distinguishing between the essential and the important helps us do just that. Only when we keep our eyes on "what we do not see," when we focus on eternal values beyond the visible, the material, and the comfortable, can we make the kind of wise choices that will keep us moving in the direction we want to go.

Question #3: What Three Activities or Responsibilities Would Make the Least Difference If I Stopped Them?

We have said that the purpose of this book is not to make you slow down. If you are overloaded, however, you may well need to cut out some activities to leave more room for the essential ones. And the place to start, of course, is to consider what activities could be eliminated with the fewest negative consequences. (If you carried out the Action Steps from the last chapter, you've already begun this process.)

Some of these might be activities that could be taken over by other people—even if there's not somebody already waiting in the wings. We need to realize that sometimes we cannot get other people to do our task simply because we continue to do it.

Every spring during my ten years of working with youth, I (Charlie) would start worrying about what we would do for leadership when the seniors graduated. I could never imagine any of the freshmen and sophomores being able to fill the seniors' shoes. But every fall, to my surprise, strong, new leaders would emerge out of the ranks of underclassmen. It was like a miracle. Once a responsibility was vacated, someone would emerge to fill it.

I have seen this happen in my own life as well. Often I have wanted to get out of a responsibility and have even asked people to take my place—but everyone said no. Then, when I stepped down anyway, someone almost always appeared to take over. My fears that nobody could fill my place proved unfounded. My letting go of the responsibility not only freed me for other things, but provided my replacement with an opportunity he or she would not otherwise have enjoyed.

Question #4: How Do the Remaining Activities Fit into My Life Purpose?

At this point, you will have determined which of your current activities are essential to you and which can easily be eliminated. This should help you determine what should go at the top and bottom of your to-do list and give you an idea what activities and responsibilities you should eliminate first. The next step is to examine the activities in the middle of the list with an eye to which ones best fit your life direction. If at all possible, these activities should remain in your life.

As the last chapter pointed out, lack of time may sometimes force you to opt out of even good activities that fit your life purpose. And responsibilities that do not fit with your life direction—even important ones—can become subtle distractions that keep you from accomplishing what you are called to do. It only makes sense, therefore, that activities that do not further your purpose should be culled out of your life.

Last fall I (Dave) had to reevaluate my activities in light of my normal struggle with my busy life. In previous years I have enjoyed making country crafts to sell in our church's Christmas Boutique. This year, however, my other responsibilities and activities had grown to the point that making enough crafts to sell would mean working in my workshop instead of going on my regular date with my wife. Because I value the time I spend with my wife, and my life purpose indicates that she is more important than making some extra money, I chose not to participate in the boutique to the extent I had in previous years.

It's a good idea, therefore, to take a look at the remaining activities and responsibilities in your life and run them through the grid of your life purpose. Ask yourself about each one, "Does this pursuit help me fulfill my purpose?" If the answer is no, we strongly suggest you begin the process of dropping that activity or responsibility.

Question #5: What Plans Do I Need to Make in Order to Stop or Get Out of My Activity/Responsibility?

It had finally become clear to me: I (Dave) had to give up my Sunday school class. I had enjoyed teaching it for the past three years. But increasing involvement in other areas of my life demanded that I give up this responsibility. The question was, how? No one was waiting in line to take my position, so I couldn't just drop it. What could I do?

What I did was develop a strategy for leaving. I was halfway through a twelve-week study. So I notified the class members and the pastor that I would teach until the end of that time, but that a new teacher should be called in to replace me afterward. During the next six weeks, I worked with the new teacher and the class leadership to make the transition smoother, but I held firm to my leaving date.

As Dave's experience with the Sunday school class shows, you cannot always get out of responsibilities immediately without doing damage. Dropping some activities responsibly might take weeks or even months. But unless you make a firm decision and develop a definite plan, you may *never* get out.

You may find it helpful, as Dave did, to set up a specific timetable for getting out of the activity or responsibility. Don't leave your plan open-ended; don't promise to stay until a replacement can be found...that might never happen. Instead, set a date for your resignation and stick to it. Then refuse any new activities or responsibilities until you have things back under control.

If you really need help in this area, try asking a close friend—perhaps your spouse—to be your clearing house for any new responsibilities. I (Charlie) have had a number of clients develop an accountability group through which they clear all new responsibilities.

Question #6: Do I Have Any "Wobble Room"?

Most of us seem to be in over our heads with activities and responsibilities. We live with chronic option overload—working at maximum capacity all the time. We leave ourselves no "wobble room," no extra space in our lives. And as a result, we have no effective way of handling negative interruptions or positive possibilities. Instead, when a crisis hits or an unforeseen opportunity arrives, we just add it to our list and hope to proceed with minimum damage. No wonder we become too hurried to love!

Time-management experts have been telling us for years not to schedule every minute of the day—to allow time for the unexpected. The same wise advice applies to life management. Instead of filling our lives to the brim, we should allow ourselves room to breathe. If we don't, we're almost certain to get ourselves into trouble.

That's what happened to me (Charlie) in the process of writing this book. My schedule was crammed—I didn't have a spare moment. Then came a call from Sylvia Nash, the executive director of the Christian Management Association. She wanted me to fill in as a speaker at their national convention in Chicago. It was a fantastic opportunity, one that would clearly further my life direction. But my pressure gauge was already on high, and there was no time to unload any of my other responsibilities. Since I had left myself no "wobble room," I had to tell Sylvia a regretful no. And I learned anew— the hard way—how important it is to leave some space in our lives.

Do yourself a favor. Go back through your list of activities and try to eliminate one more activity. If you can do that, you will be giving yourself the "wobble room" you need.

Deciding About
//////////////// ♥ **New Activities** ♥ ////////////////

If you've followed our suggested process for assessing your position, you now have a clearer idea of where you are and where you're headed. And if you were overloaded, you have "downshifted" to an appropriate speed; your pressure gauge is at an acceptable level. You even have some "wobble room" in your life.

But be prepared for new opportunities or disasters to come along and disrupt your newly achieved balance. That's just the way life is. The trick is learning how to handle new opportunities so we do not build up too much steam and again become too hurried.

Remember the egg-basket analogy we discussed in the last chapter? Even though some people have bigger baskets and seem to be able to handle more activities than others, almost all of us have baskets that are filled to the brim. Some baskets are so full that there's no room for even one little pigeon egg!

You need to think carefully, therefore, before you put any more eggs in your basket. You may find it helpful to ask yourself (and answer honestly) the following three questions about any new opportunity:

(1) *Does this activity fit my life direction?* If it does not fit, then you probably should not do it. Unless your egg basket is on the light side and you have a lot of "wobble room," you should probably say no to anything that does not promise to take you where you want to go in life.

I (Dave) tend to be a "people pleaser"; that is, I like to make people happy with me. When someone honors me by asking me to do something for them, I usually feel obligated to at least try to fit it into my already overcrowded schedule. And too often I will say yes, even if the activity doesn't further my life direction and I'm on the edge of being overwhelmed. I tell myself, "I'll make the time; I'll find a way." Instead, I end up doing a half-hearted job and feel like I've disappointed the people who trusted me. How much better it would have been to say no in the first place!

Asking myself whether or not this activity fits into my life direction is a way to distinguish between activities that fill my need to please people and those that actually further my life purpose. Having a clear life direction and staying committed to it has helped me keep my life in balance.

(2) *What egg am I going to take out of my basket to make room for this one?* If you don't ask this question about new opportunities, you are almost certain to have some breakage. One of your eggs is going to fall out—and it may be an essential one.

This question will also give you a context in which to evaluate just how wonderful this new opportunity is. Does it mean enough to you that you are willing to neglect, postpone, or sacrifice another important activity? If so, taking it on will probably be a wise choice. If not, you are better off without it. Going back and asking the "essential versus important" question can also be helpful at this point.

When approached with the opportunity to write this book, I (Charlie) had to ask the egg-basket question of myself. And when I made the decision to write the book, I actually took off two eggs to make room for it. I curtailed my part in the advancement of a consulting organization with which I was working, and I postponed starting a small-group Bible study in our neighborhood. Both these activities fit my purpose to a tee and are very important responsibilities. But I felt they both could be postponed, and the book needed to be written now.

It's important to recognize that certain responsibilities and activities in our life are nonnegotiable. Some eggs can never be taken out of our basket—they are permanent (or at least long-term) responsibilities. You never stop being a parent, for instance. You made vows of commitment to your spouse. You made a decision to follow Jesus. And you were created to have a positive influence on your friends. These nonnegotiables are by definition essentials; the activities they represent must take priority over all others. And that recognition leads to the next question:

(3) *How are my relationships with God, family, spouse, and friends?* Have you been so busy that the most significant people in your life have been neglected? What are they saying to you about the quantity and quality of time you are spending with them? Even if a new opportunity fits your life direction and you can see some activities you could drop, maybe you still need to say no.

It can sometimes be helpful to consider the relationships in our life—family, friends, and spouse—as an intricately connected system of units with God at the center. Figure 1 illustrates the relationship between these various units, which are equally important and overlap each other at many points. This means that activity in any one relationship will affect the others as well.

This means, of course, that protecting your commitment to one area of life may mean regulating your activities in another. You may need to say no to a new opportunity in one area in order to keep a balance in another area.

Business consultant Tom Peters has learned to take an evaluative look at his relationships and make sure they are doing okay before saying yes to opportunities and new responsibilities. Faced with an escalating conflict between work obligations and his family, Peters developed a set of rules to safeguard his personal priorities of family and friends.

First, he schedules no work commitments on weekends, and he accepts out-of-town engagements only on Tuesdays, Wednesdays, and Thursdays. Second, he cuts out all unnecessary meetings and social engagements. Third, he's adopted a "pay but don't go" policy to handle the many invitations to charity dinners and cultural events that seem to multiply with any professional achievement.[2] This policy takes discipline to enforce, but Peters considers such investment in his top priorities well worth the trouble.

Scheduling Your Life Around
///////////////// ♥ Relationships ♥ /////////////////

This final issue is possibly the most important in this book. It goes beyond keeping yourself on course and addresses the question of what that course should be. It assumes you have the desire to make time for the important people in your life.

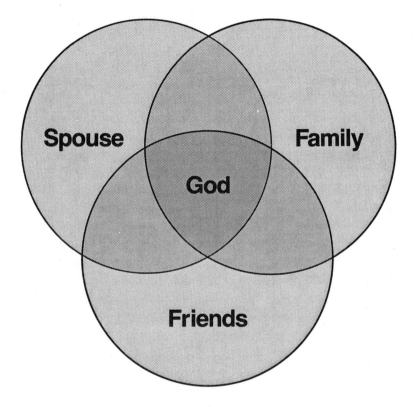

Figure 1: Relationships circles

And it makes sure that you don't take on new activities because you haven't really considered the time you need to maintain your vital relationships.

The key to having time for relationships can be found in your personal calendar. We have found that what gets on our calendar usually gets done. Your calendar, therefore, is probably where the battle against being too hurried to love will be won or lost.

Your life is no doubt besieged with urgent demands from all kinds of people. Blocking out time on your calendar for your significant relationships will help you ensure that your relationships don't get shortchanged. Make sure the special events regarding your friends are recorded. Write down that special date-night with your spouse. Then, when something else comes up, you need only check your calendar and report that you have a previous commitment.

If your relationship-centered activities are not on your calendar, chances are you will accept too many other obligations without considering the wider implications. Eventually, your well-intentioned date night becomes history. The Little League game you promised to attend gets overlooked. The dance recital for which your eight-year-old has spent the last year preparing conflicts with an important business trip. And the BBQ you planned with your friends never seems to happen. In a fast-paced world we must use our calendars as an offensive weapon.

My wife, Deb, and I (Dave) have committed to spend a half-hour on Sunday evenings to sitting with our calendars and planning our activities for the next week. We look generally at the whole month and then the quarter. We end our time together by praying for each other and the activities we'll be involved with. This little exercise has been very helpful to us in discerning what is essential and what is important in our lives.

You, too, can benefit from setting aside a consistent time to schedule essential and important activities—including relationships—on your calendar. We suggest that you schedule quarterly, monthly and weekly events:

- ♥ *Schedule quarterly:* getaway weekends, family surprises, special events, family traditions, a spiritual renewal day.

- ♥ *Schedule monthly:* whole days for God, spouse, children, friends; children's sporting events and performances; get-togethers; and even telephone calls with friends.

- ♥ *Schedule weekly:* calendar planning and date nights with spouse; regular activities with God, family, and friends—anything you want to do three to four times per week or maybe even every day.

A friend of ours who paints with water colors explained that with water colors, there is no white paint. Once the color is there, white cannot be painted over it. When preparing to paint a picture, therefore, the artist must plan the white space ahead of time. This principle is true for life as well. You must plan the white space—the time to do the essential and important relationship activities—first. And you must keep in mind that often the mistakes you make dealing with time and relationships cannot be corrected. In relationships, as in other areas of life, the people who fail to plan, plan to fail.

The process of assessing your life and keeping yourself on track that has been outlined in this chapter is a general approach—an overall plan for keeping your life from becoming overfull and making room in it for relationships. The next four chapters are designed to help you put to use the extra space you've cleared; they will help you put into practice some ideas and behaviors to enhance your relationship with God, family, and friends. We suggest that you read the next four chapters with your date book out and make quarterly, monthly, and weekly plans for healthy, thriving relationships. The planner we use is the Day-Focus System. For more information write P.O. Box 1257, San Juan Capistrano, CA 92693 or phone 1-800-662-5300.

/////////////////////////////////////// ♥ **ACTION STEPS** ♥ ///////////////////////////////////////

1. Ask yourself and three of your close friends whether you are too hurried. Are you in option overload? If in doubt, assume you are.

2. Write down the five to ten responsibilities, duties, or activities that are essential in your life.

3. Write out three to five responsibilities, duties, or activities you could stop with minimal negative effects on you and your significant others. Determine the plan necessary to curtail each of these responsibilities, duties, or activities in the next three months.

4. Refer any remaining activities to your life direction statement to see how they match up to where you want to go with your life. In light of this examination, are there any activities you can stop? If so, do it. You can always use the "wobble room."

5. Make an appointment with yourself in thirty to forty-five days to examine how you are doing in terms of making room for relationships. Get in the practice of using your calendar to make sure you do the essential things that enhance relationships.

♥

Part Four: PRACTICE

 ♥

Finding Time for God

// ♥

"God's acquaintance is not made hurriedly. He does not bestow His gifts on the casual or hasty comer and goer. To be much alone with God is the secret of knowing Him and of influence with Him."

—E.M. Bounds

"There remains, then, a Sabbath-rest for the people of God; for anyone who enters God's rest also rests from his own work, just as God did from his. Let us, therefore, make every effort to enter that rest."

—Hebrews 4:9–11

Allow me to share with you a story Lettie Cowman tells in her book, *Springs in the Valley*:

In the deep jungles of Africa, a traveler was making a long trek. Coolies had been engaged from a tribe to carry the loads. The first day they marched rapidly and went far. The traveler had high hopes of a speedy journey. But the second morning these jungle tribesmen refused to move. For some strange reason they just sat and rested. On inquiry as to the reason for this strange behavior, the traveler was informed that they had gone too fast the first day and that they were now waiting for their souls to catch up with their bodies.

Then Mrs. Cowman concludes with this penetrating exhortation:

This whirling rushing life which so many of us live does for us what that first march did for those poor jungle tribesmen. The difference: They knew what they needed to restore life's balance: too often we do not.[1]

Sound familiar? Are you feeling worn, depleted, and anxious from the pace of your life? Have you gone from being busy to being hurried? Then slow down for a moment and let the words that Jesus spoke to his weary disciples wash over your dried-out and stressed-out hearts:

Come to me, all who are weary and burdened, and I will give you rest. Take my yoke upon you and learn from me, for I am gentle and humble in heart, and you will find rest for your souls. For my yoke is easy and my burden is light. (Matt. 11:28–30)

Listen to what Jesus is saying here. He is offering us rest— and he emphasizes his offer by mentioning rest twice in this short passage. So why is the lifestyle of the average modern Christian characterized by everything but rest?

Maybe it's partly because we've neglected to fulfill Jesus' conditions for rest; we've ignored his invitation to come to him. With all the people and activities that clamor for our time, we've come to consider a quiet time with God more a luxury than a necessity. Yet if we don't come to him in a setting where we can concentrate on lifting our hearts in praise and request, we grow weary and weak—physically and emotionally, as well as spiritually.

God even gave us a whole day—the Sabbath—so we could rest and enjoy our relationship with him. Ben Patterson makes a powerful point in his book, *The Grand Essentials*:

> The Sabbath says, Stop. Look. Listen. Life is passing you by. The harder you run the more behind you get; the fuller you try to be, the more empty you become. Stop. Look. Listen. Celebrate the Sabbath. Know that you live by grace, not by work. Know that you are free. You are not a slave to necessity. Know that there is hope, that your life is moving to a grand consummation, and that it will get there by God's doing, not your own. Stop. Look. Listen.[2]

All this may seem to contradict what we've espoused through most of this book. We've been saying that it's okay to be busy—that keeping a fast pace is okay, as long as you are doing the right things and for the right reasons. But a fast pace is not the same thing as a relentless one. Your relationship with God—not to mention your well-being—*does* requires that you periodically take a break, stop, quit, cool it.

The pursuit of God requires that you make room for quiet in your life. When you're obsessing on your "to do" list, when you've given in to a compulsive need for activity, when so many voices are clamoring for your attention that you lose your perspective on what is essential, then it is easy to miss the voice of God.

God has much to say that most of us miss hearing. Because we're usually too busy or in places where the noise levels are too high, we miss his still, small voice (see 1 Kings 19:12 KJV). God will not shout to get our attention; but he does whisper to those who have made it a priority to pursue him.

One thing is certain, the pursuit of God takes time. This is one thing that cannot be rushed. The psalmist writes about waiting on the Lord all day. Jesus spent whole nights praying. Nehemiah prayed "certain days" upon hearing the plight of Jerusalem. Three times Moses spent forty days and forty nights alone with God. But in a near twenty-first-century world that demands our all just to keep up, who has that kind of time?

The idea of spending an entire day just focusing on God seems totally unrealistic to most people. But then, so does the idea of Sabbath—the "seventh day" of rest God instituted along with creation. The idea that human beings weren't designed to run full speed seven days a week and that they should take one to rest and enjoy a relationship with God sounds crazy to most people. Regrettably, the concept of Sunday being a day of rest has been lost in our hurried culture. Sunday has become a day to catch up on chores around the house, play at something just as intensely as we work, or "get a jump on Monday."

When I (Dave) talk to certain people about their quiet time with God, I sometimes get the feeling that their brains work like taxi meters that translate time and effort into money—and that they think of investing time in God's Word as less profitable than work-related activity. They talk of squeezing in a few minutes to read their Bibles before hitting the road or praying as they sit in traffic. Their spiritual nourishment reminds me of an "instant breakfast"—quick, easy, with all the basic nutrients and vitamins, but not very exciting or creative...and not really sufficient for the long haul.

Unfortunately, a meaningful, growing relationship with God rarely happens in the fast lane. Only those who slow down enough or even stop completely can hear God's voice. But oh, how most people hate to slow down! They hate even more the the idea of waiting on anything. And yet God encourages us to do both. "Be still," he urges in the Psalms, "and know that I am God" (Ps. 46:10). And another Psalm tells us to "Be still before the Lord and wait patiently for him" (Ps. 37:7).

If you find that the pace of your life makes it impossible for you to do that, then it's very possible that your lifestyle has blocked your ability to pursue God. It may be time for a change.

Making Room for
////////////// ♥ God in Your Life ♥ //////////////

What can you do on a daily basis to find enough stillness to rediscover that God is God? And what can you do to strengthen your relationship with God? Let me suggest two vital steps to having greater intimacy with God.

(1) *Find a quiet place.* Do you have a special place where you can retreat and be alone with God? If not, why not establish such a place?

Actually, you might want more than one quiet place. Establishing a spot for daily Bible study, prayer, and meditation can be tremendously effective in helping you keep up those disciplines. It may be a special chair in a quiet area of your home or office, a spot under a nearby tree, a room in a nearby church, even a hotel coffee shop after the breakfast rush has died down. The important point is that it should be a comfortable place relatively free from distractions and interruptions.

In addition, it's good to locate places where you can go for extended periods of prayer and reassessment. Retreat centers can be invaluable for this purpose, but so can hotels, parks, even the homes of friends.

In my own life (Dave), the most valuable times of intimacy with God and insight about my life direction have happened during protracted times of prayer at such places. Time spent in the gazebo at a retreat center, for instance, or long walks on the beach have been key "anchor points" in my life—times when I have made important decisions that kept my relationship with God growing.

If you're having trouble finding a place that is right for you—either for daily prayer or for spiritual retreat—make that need a subject of your prayers. Ask God to reveal a special quiet place for you and then trust him to reveal new possibilities.

(2) *Schedule time alone with God.* Setting aside daily time to be with God is a vital spiritual discipline, one that pays off richly in terms of better relationships, better focus, and a balanced approach to life. In addition, you can benefit from scheduling longer periods of time to pursue God and determine his leading in your life.

The ability to spend time in quiet meditation with God is your greatest privilege this side of heaven. Jesus Christ died on the cross to make this sort of personal communication with God possible. Because of his sacrifice on your behalf, you can now come into the presence of God, boldly holding out your needs before him.

Tips for Building
a Closer Relationship
///////////////////// ♥ **with God** ♥ /////////////////////

In the following pages we would like to share some ideas about some things you can do during your time alone with God. These are tools and ideas that have helped us focus on the person of God and build a deeper relationship with him. Some are appropriate for daily use, others more suited for extended periods of time. We urge you to try one or two of these suggestions and see if they encourage you in your own walk with God.

Keeping a Journal

For a long time I (Dave) resisted the discipline of journaling. My reasoning was that it took too much time and would slow down the time I spent with God. Then I began to notice that every godly person I knew or read about had kept a journal about God's working in their lives. That's when I began a discipline that has been fully as helpful as learning to read in coming to know God and his ways.

Why has journaling been such a powerful tool in my life? Let me suggest a few important reasons:

(1) *A journal helps me remember.* The habit of writing down my feelings and experiences keeps me in touch with how God has moved in my past to lead and provide for me. Recording the times when the miraculous has happened in my life gives me something to go back to when the days are dark and my faith is weak.

(2) *A journal sharpens my thinking.* The process of writing clarifies my mind and helps me sort out the important issues from the ones that simply distract me. My pen has become one of my the most important thinking tools.

(3) *A journal slows me down.* What I thought would be a drag on my time with God has turned out to be one of the most beneficial aspects. The process of writing out my reflections and my prayers has caused me really to think about what I am

doing with my life and my faith. I can no longer slide easily past a scripture or a life event that God wants to use to grab my attention.

(4) *A journal helps me examine my life.* A wise man once shared with me the words of Socrates: "The unexamined life is not worth living." Viewed from that perspective, my journal helps keep my life worthwhile. Writing down my mistakes and my failures helps keep me from repeating those errors. It also helps me develop a clearer long-term perspective; I can see how God can use even my bad moves for good in my life.

If by now I've managed to convince you to start a journal, let me offer some tips for getting started:

- ♥ *Don't let the blank page intimidate you.* Write today's date and begin with the word *Yesterday....* Then just write whatever comes to your head.

- ♥ *Turn off the editor in your head.* Don't worry about proper spelling or grammar. Don't go back and reread or make corrections until you are completely finished. Chances are, no one will ever read your journal but you. Relax and let it be an honest account of what you are thinking and feeling.

- ♥ *Limit yourself to one page.* This will help you tighten up your thoughts and keep you from rambling.

- ♥ *Write when you want to... but try to stay consistent.* Some people prefer to have a set time for journaling, but others do better by writing when they feel like writing.

- ♥ *Keep your journals for future reference.* Looking back at your past journals is one of the best possible ways to clarify where you have been, where you are going, and how God has worked in your life.

Spend a Day with God

Unless you intentionally plan to spend an extended time with God, you'll never manage it. Even the best plans can be foiled, of course, but having no plan means you'll never have the opportunity. Take your calendar out now and mark out the better part of a day in a quiet place praying, reading, and listening to God. Plan to spend this kind of prolonged and undistracted time with God on a regular basis. Be realistic, but work hard to make room in your busy schedule for the protracted times of fellowship and conversation with God.

Get Away to a Christian Camp

Being in a natural setting like the mountains, the beach, the woods, or the lake can help inspire and renew your passion for God. Many Christian conference centers are located in beautiful settings and offer both weekend retreats and week-long camps. Natural surroundings, inspirational music, good speakers, and a prepared heart can combine to make a memorable event. You might think of time spent at these Christian camps as vacations with a purpose.

Last Thanksgiving, for example, my wife, my kids, and I (Charlie) spent the weekend at a special family camp in the mountains nearby. The two outstanding speakers and the forested environment made those three days a time of spiritual renewal for us as well as a rewarding time of family togetherness. We've even talked about making Thanksgiving in the mountains a family tradition.

Try a Correspondence with God

Picture yourself walking up to your mailbox and finding a letter with no return address. You rip it open and are stunned to find it is a letter from God. At first you think it's just a joke, but the words have a ring of truth. What does it say?

On one sheet of paper, write what you think God would be saying to you if he wrote such a letter. You might find it helpful to follow the format of the letters God told John to write to the seven churches in Revelation (Rev. 1:19–3:22):

1. A personalized greeting

2. A special name God has given himself

3. Some good news—praise for a Christian virtue

4. Some bad news—blame for a specific sin

5. A request for change

6. A warning of what will happen if the request is ignored

7. A promise of what will happen if the change is made[3]

This exercise can do wonders to help you sharpen your listening skills and understand what God wants for your life. You may find it especially helpful as a way of "tuning in" to God and preparing to develop a life-direction statement from chapter 2 or a "position assessment" process outlined in chapter 6.

The mail can go both ways, of course. Before or after you write out your letter from God, try writing a letter *to* God. (This can be part of your journal or a separate project.) Tell him what is happening in your life—what brings you joy and what causes discouragement. Write down your dreams and your future plans.

Writing letters to and from God is really a way of praying on paper. You may find it tremendously helpful in keeping you focused and alert and clarifying your thoughts and perceptions. Keep your letters for future reference. Like your journal, they will provide you with exciting evidence of God's work in your life.

Keep a Prayer List

Writing down your requests to God serves much the same purpose as writing a letter to God. It provides you with tangible evidence of God's work in your life, as well as reminding you of key areas of concern.

Keep your list in a special area of your journal. You don't have to pray through the list every day, but do add to it and review it on a regular basis. And when your prayers are answered, take the time to record the answer next to the request. People who have tried this discipline are almost always excited to see how God answers their petitions. Much of the time, we miss the blessing of seeing our prayers answered simply because we have not taken the trouble to write them down.

Make a "Remember When" List

Another helpful list to keep in your journal is a record of God's supernatural workings in your life. Write out all the significant times God has answered your prayer or directed your life and circumstances. There will, of course, be some overlap with your prayer list, but the emphasis will be slightly different.

If you work to keep your "remember when" list current, you will quickly see that God is alive and well. You will also have a powerful source of encouragement for periods when your faith falters. Next time you find yourself doubting God's love for you, go back to your list. The evidence that God cares for you and guides you will be right there in your own handwriting.

Sanctify Your Cassette Player

Are you a commuter? Rather than listening to just any radio station or cassette on your way to work, try playing Christian music and inspirational or self-help tapes. The time you spend commuting can be transformed into a time of praise and prayer—with your eyes open, of course! The same can be true on any kind of extended automobile trip. Many people find that playing Christian tapes on headsets while walking or jogging (again, keeping safety in mind) can provide daily encouragement and edification.

Take the Word with You

If you take the trouble to memorize verses of Scripture, you can then take the Bible with you wherever you go and call upon its help at any time. Memorizing even one verse a month will help your understanding of God and aid you in sensing his presence.

Try writing out a verse or short passage on a card during your quiet time and then rereading it over the course of the day until you've committed it to memory. Over the period of a few months, you will have stored a significant portion of God's word in your memory.

Building a Relationship
///////////////////////// ♥ **with God** ♥ /////////////////////////

Your relationship with God is just that—a relationship. And like any other relationship, it will require time, planning, and nurturing. The time you invest in keeping that relationship vital will pay a thousand times more in terms of keeping your whole life vital, meaningful, and unhurried.

Make time today to spend quality time with God. Experiencing his love on a regular basis is one of the most important things you can do to avoid becoming too hurried to love.

///////////////////////// ♥ **ACTION STEPS** ♥ /////////////////////////

1. Locate a quiet place free of interruption where you can get away on a regular basis to be with God.

2. Look over your weekly schedule and find times where you can get away to your quiet place to be with God.

3. Look over your quarterly calendar. When can you set aside time to spend the better part of a day with God?

   Date: _____ Day: _____ Time: _____

4. Purchase a simple notebook—spiral, loose-leaf, or whatever you are comfortable with—and begin keeping a journal. Start by writing down the word "Yesterday" and let your pen flow.

5. In your journal, begin keeping track of God's miraculous work in your life. One way to do this is to keep an ongoing prayer list to remind you of what to pray and a record of how God answers. Reading over this list at the end of the year can be one of the most encouraging things you do during your New Year's celebration.

Friends for a Lifetime

/// ♥

*"Two are better than one, because they have a good
return for their work: if one falls down, his friend can
help him up. But pity the man who falls and has no one to
help him up!"*

—Ecclesiastes 4:9,10

*"I've had one or two people who have been lifelong
friends. I think friendship is probably the most beautiful
of all human relationships, because even what is called
love in the physical sense has a certain self interest. But a
friendship is not that way. It is a very precious element in
life."*

—Malcolm Muggeridge

There is nothing quite like a funeral to bring you back in
touch with the things that really matter.

I (Dave) laid a good friend to rest not long ago. Brent was
thirty-one years old, in the prime of life, run down by an out-
of-control driver while he changed a flat tire on the roadside.
And as I stood by his freshly dug grave remembering him, the
legacy of his life suddenly shifted into sharp focus. What
mattered on that day was not that Brent had been a great
plumber, but that he had been a great friend. No one cared

whether he had amassed any wealth; what people cared about was that he had spent extravagant amounts of time building memories with his children. What kind of car he drove, what position he had attained in life, how much fame he had acquired—none of these things seemed important. No, what mattered now was that he had loved his wife with a passion, his kids with all his affections, his friends with his substance, and his God with all his heart, mind, and strength.

As I looked at that grave, I was reminded that all Brent was able to leave me with was memories...but that was enough. For the rest of my life I will remember the relationship I had with Brent and look forward to the one I will have with him later in the kingdom of God.

Brent's death made me ask myself some hard questions—questions like:

- ♥ "What's happened to me? When did I decide to spend so much time pursuing the things that don't last rather than investing myself in people who will live eternally?"

- ♥ "How come I've allowed the fun of normal living to be snuffed out by my desire to acquire things, be the best, or attain a powerful position in life?"

- ♥ "Whoever convinced me that I should feel guilty if I take time away from my work to make a memory with someone that I love?"

- ♥ "Why did it take the death of a friend for me to wise up?"

Increasingly I became aware of the many individuals around me who were allowing themselves to miss out on the richness of meaningful friendships. I began to notice that most of these people could be characterized as *busy people*.

The Busy Life and the
///////////// ♥ Relationship Drain ♥ /////////////

Busy people are people on the go. They are the ones who are heavily involved with a number of worthwhile activities—jobs, family, church, hobbies, civic organizations, and charitable foundations—in addition to the mundane tasks of maintaining cars and homes, buying clothes, and cooking food. Busy people tend to have many acquaintances. People seem attracted to them—perhaps because busy people seem more interesting. Busy people tend to make things happen, so life becomes exciting when they are around.

And yet we have observed that, although busy people tend to be surrounded by "friends," they typically lack the kind of intimate relationship one would call "a best friend" or even a "close friend." We believe this happens because, rather than investing time in developing a profound connection with a few people, the busy person prefers to fill his or her relationship needs through surface acquaintance with a lot of people.

A few years ago, I (Dave) personally came to a point where I realized that most of my friendships were either with people who needed to plug into me (the draining type) or people whom I knew only on a very surface level. Although I spent a lot of my time with people, I found myself starving for a close mutual friendship. I asked around, and I discovered that many other people had the same sort of feelings, although they had a hard time describing just what a "close friend" should be.

How would you describe your friendships? Do you tend to have many acquaintance-level friends, a smaller circle of close but not intimate friends, just one or two old friends you would trust with your life? The rest of this chapter is designed to help you understand how your friendships work and give you some ideas for making more time in your life for quality friendships.

﹀﹀ ♥ Your Friendship Circle ♥ ﹀﹀

Friendship has many possible varieties and encompasses many levels. Think of all the different kinds of friends you have. To some you would give your last dollar. With others you might only drink coffee. Some you seek out when you have particular needs, and others you try to avoid at certain times. Classmates, co-workers, pastors, teachers, mechanics, clerks, buddies, and soul mates all make up what could be called your friendship circle.

You may find it helpful to think of these many levels of friendship as a series of concentric circles, as shown in figure 2. Keep in mind, however, that no analogy is perfect. The point of analyzing your friendships is not to pigeonhole people or rate your relationships—they will probably shift with time and circumstance. Instead, we hope you will use the diagram as a help in understanding how friendships develop and as a guide for developing deeper, more intimate relationships with your friends.

F-1 Friends

The people in your "inside circle" of friendship are what we would call your F-1 friends (F = friend). When we describe an F-1 friend, we're talking about someone who is neither overly impressed with your strengths nor devastated by your weakness. F-1s are people with whom you can be yourself, people with whom you have chosen to share your deepest feelings and dreams. They know you at your core because you have chosen to be absolutely honest with them. They are the people who meet you at the point when your need for friendship is greatest. And they are the ones you most look forward to being with.

Interestingly, F-1 friends rarely turn out to be people you

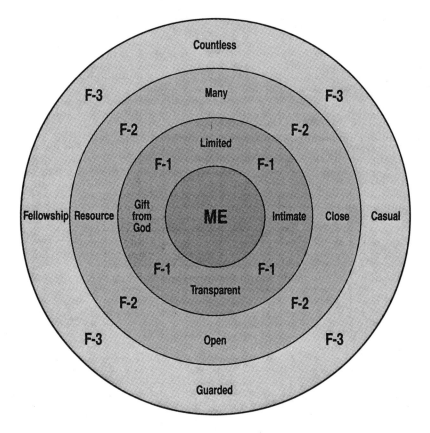

Figure 2: Friendship circle

have deliberately recruited to be your friends. Instead, God draws you together in a miraculous way and gives feelings of mutual attraction. These friendships, therefore, are truly gifts from God. They have a lasting quality which develops into a bond over the years.

Obviously, one cannot nurture more than two or three F-1 friends at once; time simply prohibits it. For these are the kind of friendships you have to cultivate with care over the years. F-1 friends are the ones with whom you check in at different points during the week, the ones you seek out for long hours of conversation. Such friends are the kind of people you would list as your most treasured possession; you'll want to take special care with them.

We believe that developing a few specially chosen F-1s is of far more value than being so popular that you receive enough Christmas cards each year to wallpaper the bathroom. Our relationships with our F-1 friends energize us. They makes us more optimistic and hopeful. We find it is a joy to be with our F-1 friends even in times of sorrow. Time with F-1 friends should be given the highest priority.

F-2 Friends

F-2 friends are people you enjoy being with—true friends in the sense of loyalty and support. They know you and like you, and you enjoy being with them. F-2s are the kind of friends you see regularly in the course of living. They include your colleagues at work, your fellow church members, your neighbors, classmates, and many others. You see them almost every day. You wish them well. You know something about their lives. But either because you have not known them long enough, because the "chemistry" is not there, or because for some reason they are unavailable, you have never been able to really "unpack your bags" with them.

One person could maintain many F-2 friendships at a time—anywhere from twenty to a hundred or more—and these friendships may last for a few months or a lifetime. The number and duration depends both on your personality and on your circumstances. If you are basically outgoing and active in getting to know people, your list of F-2 friends is likely to be long. And this is especially true if you move frequently or become involved in a variety of opportunities— the wider the circles in which you move, the more F-2 friends you are likely to have. And the more F-2 friends we have the greater demand on our time. It becomes important to realize one cannot spend the same amount of time with all their friends. Again F-1 friends need to be our priority.

F-3 Friends

F-3s are low-maintenance friends. Psychologist Rollo May has done research that suggests that most people will make five hundred to twenty-five hundred of these casual acquaintances each year.[1] F-3s are the kind of people that surround your life but don't really touch it deeply. They are the people you speak to at work or church but rarely spend much time with. You know who they are, but you know little about how they actually live or think. You would say that you know them or that they are friends of yours, but you never have had the opportunity or the inclination to spend much time with them. And that is okay. Not all relationships are equal. We have acquaintances (F-3), important relationships (F-2), and essential friends (F-1).

▒▒ ♥ A Friend-Poor Society ♥ ▒▒

We all need friends at every level, F-1s, F-2s, and F-3s, to live a happy life. Unfortunately, the friendship circle of most adults consists only of a multitude of F-3s and a few F-2s. This is especially true for men. Rarely do we observe men who are intentionally nurturing F-1 relationships. Maybe that's because maintaining F-1 friendships requires a willingness to share openly about oneself and many men shy away from such openness.

In many ways, we live in a society that shortchanges deep friendship. We are a fiercely independent generation in a cultural tradition that stresses independence and autonomy. We are also a hurried generation—stressed out, overloaded, and on the run. And all these things can create a roadblock against the kind of deep relationships for which human beings were created.

Many people are so stressed out from the daily demands placed on them that all they want to do is hide away within the confines of their home and enjoy their own space. (Futures consultant Faith Popcorn calls this "stay at home" phenomenon "cocooning.") People drive away from their houses early in the morning, work all day at their office, and return that evening without saying a word to their next-door neighbor. A push of a button and the garage door goes up; they never even have to get out of their car before disappearing into their private domain.

In such an atmosphere, friendships are not actively sought; if they do happen they are more unintentional than planned. And intimate friendships rarely develop that way. There is no quick or haphazard way to grow an F-1 friendship. These kinds of relationships develop at their own pace, often over a long period of time.

We believe, in fact, that the primary reason F-1s are not commonly developed is that few people find themselves in settings intense enough to create them. F-1 friendships are usually *forged,* not developed casually; they grow out of intense experiences we've shared with other people. That explains why friendships developed under the stress of military combat or in other crisis situations tend to be stronger and deeper than other friendships. It might also explain why you have maintained close contact with a friend that went through college or graduate school with you and why you married the person you did. (Yes, your spouse can be your most important F-1 friend.)

If God designed the universe so that the only things that will last forever are himself and people, then relationships are the most valuable commodities human beings can have on this earth. Yet the demanding lifestyle so many people have chosen leaves little time or energy to put into relationships. Maybe all of us need to challenge that thinking and reconsider our priorities to make more room for friendship in our lives.

The Benefits
////////////// ♥ of Friendships ♥ //////////////

Both of us feel quite blessed when it comes to the subject of friendship. We can point to certain individuals whom we would consider to be friends at each level, and we are grateful for all of them. Let us list just a few of the benefits we have personally experienced from our relationship with the men and women who have been willing to be our friends:

(1) *Help and encouragement.* Our friendships have brought joy and hope into our life during some dark days.

At one point in my life (Dave), the church I was serving as an associate pastor fell apart. I was caught in the middle of a very ugly situation and without an income to support a wife and two young children. During that time, my friends stood by and helped, often at great personal expense. Some of my most treasured F-1 friends were born in those days of adversity.

(2) *Stability.* Our friends give us roots. We are at home in our community because it's where our friends live. We feel comfortable worshiping in our churches because it's where our friends worship. Our friends know us and we know them. There is a mutuality in our familiarity. They form a foundation for a stable life.

(3) *Wisdom and accountability.* Our friends keep us from making rash decisions that could destroy us or hurt others. Some of my friends—especially my F-1 friends—know me so well they can sit across that coffee-shop table, look me right in the eye, and say "Dave, what you're saying is hogwash." They care deeply enough about me to speak the truth in love and to provide me with the honest evaluation I need to make midcourse corrections in my life directions.

(4) *Spiritual help.* We love the proverb "As iron sharpens iron, so one man sharpens another" (Prov. 27:17). This has been true for us in terms of spiritual growth; our friends have provided our greatest motivation and help in this area. They encourage us to excel as spiritual leaders and inspire us to grow deeper in our devotion to Christ.

(5) *A sense of being loved.* Even the most self-confident people need to know that someone loves and accepts them. Our friends love us just the way we are—not because of our professional standing or prestige in the community, not because we're funny or cute, not because of what we've done, but just because we're who we are—and they make sure we know that they love us. The confidence their love gives us goes beyond words. They quench our fear of rejection.

(6) *Someone to love.* True friendship is a two-way street. Our friends give us opportunities to give back what we have received from them. In so doing, they allow us the satisfaction that comes with giving. If all we did was receive, we would not enjoy the sense of mutual respect that comes from a reciprocal relationship. We are peers, equals with our friends; we meet with the sense that all of us bring something of value to the table.

⁄⁄⁄⁄⁄⁄⁄ ♥ Fostering Friendship ♥ ⁄⁄⁄⁄⁄⁄⁄

As we have seen, friendships develop under many different circumstances—some of which we cannot control. But there is a lot we *can* do to increase our chances of making friends and to nurture the friendships we already have. Consider adding some of these activities to your lifestyle:

Join a Group—or Start One

Each week, I (Dave) meet with a small group of people who encourage me, inspire me, listen to me, even correct me— who above all else like being with me. I like being with them too. The value of such an accountability group is that it is a place where one can know others and be known.

Small groups can be composed of couples, singles, men and women—any combination of people. But there is a special dynamic that can take place in a small group when each member is of the same sex. Sharing can be more candid and empathy usually runs deep.

Some of the most effective groups are those whose members meet to help each other with a shared problem—using the power of friendship to bring out the best in each other. Drug and alcohol recovery groups, overcomers groups, and a myriad of other kinds of support groups qualify as places where friends fight their personal battles in the context of encouragement.

Write a Note

Never discount the power of the written word. Note writing may be the most effective use of the time you invest in growing a friendship. Writing down your thoughts about someone in the form of a short note is a tangible expression of your love and concern. A word of advice: Notes don't need to be long or poetic to be endearing. A few lines that express your thanks or tell someone you were thinking about him or her can speak volumes. A well-timed word of encouragement can do wonders for a sagging friendship and help get a budding relationship off the ground.

Go on an Adventure Together

Getting away together to do something exciting or adventurous can be a wonderful friendship builder. Intentionally testing your limits and going through a difficult experience can bring you closer and help you really know each other. River rafting, mountain climbing, long-distance bicycling, backpacking—or just going on the road—can all be good bonding experiences for friends.

Work Out or Play Together

Any kind of common sporting activity that can be done on a consistent basis—walking, tennis, golf, aerobics—can be a great way to build a friendship. A membership in a health or athletic club can be a great way to build good relationships. And walking or jogging together can provide the double benefit of safety and enhanced friendship.

Retreat Together

Taking time away from the hustle of life to just spend time together can be a great investment in your friendship. Rent a cabin in the mountains for the weekend to ski or fish. Five women I know reserve a hotel suite once a year for a weekend to do nothing but talk together.

Lend a Hand

A true test of friendship is a willingness to help another at his or her point of need—and helping one another is a proven relationship builder. Do you know someone who could use a hand moving, painting their house, fixing their car? Maybe you could give (not loan) a friend some money to help ease them through a difficult time. Friends look for ways to help each other.

Another form of helping that can build wonderful friendships is working together on a project to help someone else. Volunteer together for a church workday. Team up on a community-wide program to fix houses for the elderly or feed the homeless. Join forces to chaperone a youth mission trip. The satisfaction of helping those in need and the camaraderie of working together can quickly deepen a relationship.

Throw a Party

Don't wait for a holiday or a birthday to give a party. All the reason you need for a celebration is a desire to be together. For a special touch of nostalgia, invite some friends who have moved out of your area back for a reunion.

Share a Meal

Something special happens when a friend joins you at your

house or apartment for dinner. You don't need to make anything fancy to eat or deep-clean the place. Just being with each other is what counts. To stimulate conversation, try some of the discussion starters we list in chapter 9.

Reach Out and Touch

Your telephone is a splendid tool for maintaining both your local and your long-distance friendships. And long-distance doesn't cost as much as you think. For much less than the cost of a fast-food dinner, you can talk to an out-of-state friend for half an hour or more. You can usually manage a phone call even when you don't have the time for a coffee-shop meeting or writing a letter. While telephone contact should not become a substitute for written communication or face-to-face conversation, it can do wonders to keep your friendship connections fresh. (One woman told us that the first thing she did after reading an early version of this chapter was to call her best friend three states away!)

Have a Friend By
//////////////// ♥ **Being a Friend** ♥ ////////////////

If you want to have friends, you must show yourself to be friendly, so the saying goes. We develop friendships, in other words, by *being* friends to others—and by working to develop our capacity for friendships.

Initiating friendships is easier for some people than for others, of course. If you are naturally gregarious, you probably find it easy to make new friends—but you might also need to concentrate on nurturing the ones you have. If you are the shy type or just a loner, you may have learned to nurture deep friendships with one or two, but you might have to push yourself a little to develop new ones.

In either case, the point is not to change your basic personality, but to build on your relational strengths and improve your relational weaknesses with the purpose of developing a rich, well-balanced friendship network. We believe you will find that enriched friendships make all your efforts worthwhile.

/// ♥ **ACTION STEPS** ♥ ///

1. Write down the names of the three people with whom you want to spend more time this year:

   1. _____

   2. _____

   3. _____

2. Which of the suggestions made at the end of this chapter will you invite these people to follow with you? Write them down in your notebook.

3. Spend some time right now praying for your F-1 friends. If you feel you don't have any F-1 friends, make that need the focus of your prayer.

4. If you are not currently involved in a small group, begin making plans to do so. Write out a list of possible groups you're aware of. If none of these seem viable, ask a pastor or friend for suggestions.

5. Take the time to express your feelings to a friend on paper. Your note doesn't have to be long; just jot down your thoughts on a note card. Be sure to mail it!

Keeping the Romance Alive

// ♥

"Marriage ... is not so much finding the right person as being the right person."

—Charlie Shedd

"A great lover is someone who can satisfy one woman all her life long ... and who can be satisfied by one woman all his life long. A great lover is not someone who goes from woman to woman. Any dog can do that."

—An actor well-known for his romantic roles, speaking candidly on a late-night talk show.

"You husbands ... live with your wives in an understanding way."

—1 Peter 3:7 NASB

Before Greg and Julie were married, they spent every minute they could with each other. If they couldn't participate in a recreational activity together, neither of them would spend time doing it. They even found themselves putting off some of their favorite activities because it sounded like more fun just to be together. Their work, which previously had absorbed most of their energies, took second place in their

lives; they never allowed it to interfere with their time together in the evenings. Greg's job sometimes required him to
travel. But on the evenings he was away, they would call each
other and sometimes talk for hours. Communication was
never a problem; there seemed to be so much to talk about.

Sometimes Julie would find, under the wiper blade of her
car, a single red rose with a love note attached. On occasion, she would prepare Greg a candlelight dinner in her
apartment with just the right music softly playing in the
background.

But in the first few years after Julie and Greg were married,
some changes took place in their relationship. Although they
now lived in the same house, it seemed they actually spent
less time together. Moonlit walks on the beach were largely a
thing of the past; cards and notes were reserved for holidays;
and dinners out were primarily for eating, not talking. When
Greg traveled, he would call once or twice to check in, but
they would keep the calls short to save money on their bill.
Julie and Greg could tell they were spending much less time
and attention on each other.

Once the children started coming, Julie and Greg found
their life even more practical and less romantic. Now the
children's needs were the focus of every evening—that is,
when Julie could drag Dave away from the television to help
her with the kids. They both fell into bed each night too
exhausted for anything beside a peck on the cheek.

Before Julie and Greg were married, they couldn't get
enough time together. Now their lives were filled with the
concerns and pressures of everyday life. Preoccupation with
finances, the kids, the house, the car, and a million other
details had snuffed out the joy of being in love. In fact, if Julie
and Greg were really honest, each would have to admit that
they were now more like roommates than they were lovers.

Does this scenario sound painfully familiar? If so, let us give you some good news. Romance *can* flourish in your busy world. All it takes is the "want to"—plus some good, old-fashioned hard work.

Why isn't the "want to" enough? Because motivation tends to wane once a relationship is established. When a relationship is new, the "want to" is extremely high. Greg and Julie were willing to cancel appointments in favor of the relationship. They spent whole days and evenings in pursuit of each other. Their energy seemed boundless, and money was never a concern.

So what changed after marriage? Reality hit. The "want to" turned into "I forgot to" or "I don't have time to," and gradually the flames of love began to die down.

In order for love to grow, both partners must have a commitment to work on the "want to," to continue adding fuel to the fire. And that's where the hard work comes in. Married people who want to keep romance in their marriage must *work* at keeping it alive. Contrary to popular opinion, a vital, exciting relationship doesn't just happen. It has to be nurtured and cherished, verbalized and discussed, protected and encouraged.

I love what author Walter Trobisch said about love:

> Love is a feeling to be learned.
> It is tension and fulfillment.
> It is gladness and it is pain.
> There is not one without the other.
> Happiness is only part of love.
> This is what has to be learned.
> Suffering belongs to love also.
> This is the mystery of love,
> Its beauty and its burden.
> Love is a feeling to be learned.[1]

Like anything else you learn, romance in marriage takes all the time and effort you have to give it...and more. But most people we talk to say they have little time and little energy left at the end of the day to devote to being romantic. Maybe that feeling alone explains why the divorce rate is so high among professional working couples. Romance dies when it is neglected.

Being in love is not a static thing. It is the nature of love to be everchanging—to ebb and flow with the seasons of our lives. A man who says, "I told her I loved her when I married her; I'll let her know if anything changes" doesn't understand that a healthy romantic relationship demands attention—a lot of attention.

The Ingredients of a
//////////////// ♥ **Vital Marriage** ♥ ////////////////

There are five elements that we consider critical to keeping marriage meaningful and satisfying and keeping the romance in marriage. We believe that if you take us seriously and apply these concepts to any marriage, your efforts can effect noticeable change in a relatively short period.

Rule #1: Give Each Other Time

To accomplish anything in your relationship, you must reserve time for the relationship. And we mean "quality time"—time when you can give the marriage your undivided attention.

But how much time are we talking about? That depends on the condition of the relationship. If your marriage is healthy, it will probably need less time than if you are on the verge of divorce or entangled in an affair and need to do some major repair work. A good rule of thumb would be two hours of undivided attention each day. We also recommend setting aside regular time to go out on dates together. (We will discuss this in more detail later in the chapter.)

It's incredible how many couples I (Dave) counsel try to talk me out of this rule. They argue that there is no way they can find the time to invest in romance. Some workaholic spouses argue that their work just takes up too much time. My question is: How can so many of these men and women find time for an extramarital affair? The same person who can't get home for dinner with the family can manage an afternoon escape three times a week.

Most couples—even very busy ones—*can* find the time to keep romance in their lives; it's simply a matter of priorities. And making time for one another may be the single most important thing you can do to keep your relationship vital.

Rule #2: Make an Effort at Communication

Most experts agree that meaningful communication is the key to a lasting and satisfying marriage. Meaningful communication is more than "Did you feed the cat today?" or "How much money is in the checkbook?" Meaningful communication is sharing with each other your heartfelt thoughts and desires concerning a wide range of topics.

According to at least one study, the average married couple in America spends less than twenty minutes per week in meaningful communication, but more than twenty hours per week watching TV. Maybe the solution to the lack of romantic love in your marriage would be to turn off the TV and just talk!

Touch may be one of the most effective forms of communication. Touching your mate as you talk with him or her communicates understanding, care, and acceptance. Eye contact is also a form of touch—an extremely powerful one. Next time you talk to your spouse, try looking straight into his or her eyes while holding hands. We think you'll like the response. Eye contact and a gentle touch says to your spouse, "You have my full attention."

Rule #3: Give Each Other Grace

A wise man said, "Grace is the oil that keeps a marriage running smoothly." To give another person grace is to extend kindness to someone who doesn't deserve it. We believe that our ability to forgive each other for little hurts and inappropriate comments has been a critical factor in holding together our respective marriages. Without it, the tendency is to lay blame, assess guilt, and place fault.

Rule #4: Encourage Each Other

Probably the most powerful words that can be spoken in a marriage are those of encouragement. Words of criticism create feelings of anger and defensiveness. But encouragement lifts us up and gives us confidence and assurance. Actress Celeste Holm once said, "We live by encouragement and without it we die, slowly, sadly and angrily." She was right. There is no way to know just how many people are dying slowly, sadly, and angrily in their marriages, but you can be sure that the number is astronomical. One look at the divorce statistics will confirm that at least half the people who are married are not happy in their marriages. And we believe the lack of mutual encouragement contributes to this unhappiness. How different things would be if only married people would make an effort to become encouragers!

We suggest that you deliberately make the time to encourage your spouse each day. In some special way, recognize the good in him or her. Maybe it's just letting your wife know how fortunate you feel that she married you. Or telling your husband he looks great in those clothes. How about recognizing your spouse's success in his or her chosen profession or his or her courage in changing professions?

Encouraging one another is really easy if you put your mind to it. So make the effort to encourage your spouse. You'll like the way it pays off in your marriage.

////////// ♥ Start Dating Again! ♥ *//////////*

Most married couples we talk to have dating lives that have fallen into a rut or even into the dumpster! In our experience, couples who have been married longer than five years seldom spend time together like they did while they were courting. We think that's a tragedy! Good, well-meaning people are missing the joy that comes from being in love—and their marriages are missing out on the strengthening that regular, concentrated time together can bring.

A few years ago, my wife and I (Dave) were out doing some grocery shopping. A young man who worked at the store took one look at our expressionless faces and asked, "Hey, are you guys married?" "I thought so," he remarked when we replied affirmatively. "You look married." Needless to say, that caused us some alarm. We had confirmed his observation that married couples tend to be bored with one another and do boring things with their lives. Unfortunately, he was right. Our relationship *had* gone stale. So we decided to do something about it. We began going out on a date together once week. And renewing our "dating relationship" has done wonders for our marriage.

Allow us to share with you some principles we think might make a difference as you renew your dating life:

(1) *Go out without the kids.* Children can deeply enrich your marriage and deepen your relationship—but you also need time just for the two of you. Children are by definition demanding of your time and attention. If they are with you constantly, they can keep you from focusing your attention on each other. We recommend, if all possible, that you arrange to be without your children for a few hours each week.

(2) *Keep your date night dependable.* Under the pressure of a busy lifestyle, it's easy to get into the habit of letting your date nights slide. One way to fight this tendency is to eliminate some of the common excuses—"Can't get a sitter," "Something came up," "We don't have the money!"—ahead of time. This will probably mean setting a regular time when neither of you has commitments, marking it on both your calendars, and making arrangements for reliable and regular child care.

Deb and I (Dave) chose a night when we knew we would be free at least 95 percent of the time and found a sitter we could count on being at our house every week. Then we adjusted our budget to free up funds for child care and an inexpensive date. As a result, we are much less likely to have our date night co-opted or interrupted.

(3) *Learn not to include friends on a date.* An evening with other couples is fun, but it doesn't do much to further your romantic relationship. Always keep in mind the reasons you are dating—to get you out together and encourage romance.

(4) *Choose activities where you can give each other your undivided attention.* Movies, television, spectator sports, and similar activities are old standbys for dates. But you can't

really give each other your undivided attention while watching a movie, a TV sitcom, or a baseball game. For this reason, although such activities are fine once in a while, they shouldn't be your dating mainstays. Instead, look for activities that give you the opportunity to pay close attention to each other. The last part of this chapter gives some specific suggestions.

(5) *Stay off the well-traveled conversational paths.* We've found that talking about kids or finances never leads to a happy conversation on our dates. For this reason, we have proclaimed those subjects to be off-limits during our nights out with our spouses. When we share this with others, they sometimes respond by asking sincerely, "What else is there to talk about?" Here are some conversation starters:

- ♥ "Tell me something I don't know about you" (a great request for your silver anniversary).

- ♥ "What do you think are the three most romantic times we have spent together?"

- ♥ "With what movie star or sports figure would you most like to talk for an hour? Why?"

- ♥ "How would you describe your ideal vacation?"

- ♥ "If you only had six months to live, but would be in no physical pain, what would you do?"

- ♥ "What event or situation brings a tear to your eye the quickest?"

- ♥ "What is the most meaningful compliment you have received in the last twelve months?"

- ♥ "Who was your favorite teacher in school? Why?"

- ♥ "What are your three fondest memories of your teenage years?"

- ♥ "Who do you consider your three or four closest personal friends? Why?"

- ♥ "What is a key to 'turning you on'? Is there anything I have been missing?"

- ♥ "Do you evaluate a day according to how much you enjoyed it or how much you accomplished?"

- ♥ "What did you learn about marriage from watching your parents that you find helpful now?"

We haven't found staying off the conversational no-nos to be a problem in our dating lives. In fact, we predict that once you determine to stay off your most heavily traveled roads of conversation, you will probably discover countless fascinating side roads to explore together. In the process, you may learn things you never knew about one another.

Romance Boosters for
///////////// ♥ **Married People** ♥ /////////////

For the past seven years, Deb and I (Dave) have made dating a priority and it has revolutionized our marriage. Tuesday nights with Deb are something I have come to look forward to each week. I plan to continue making our marriage a dating relationship for many years to come.

But dating regularly is just one of the ways you can keep the spark in your marriage. Here are some other ideas for renewing the interest and excitement in your relationship with the person you loved enough to marry. You can try out some of these ideas on your dates together or you use them to surprise one another in the midst of your everyday living:

Putting Your Romance on Paper

Just for a moment, think about your spouse. What are the qualities you admire, respect, or are grateful for? What does he or she do well? What strengths of character does he or she display? What do you think is physically attractive about your husband or wife. In a love note, list twenty-one reasons you love your mate. Love-note writing is just that easy.

The art of communicating love on paper is rapidly going the way of the dinosaur in our high-tech culture. We think this is unfortunate, because written expressions of love have some clear advantage over spoken ones. Putting your love on paper provides you with an opportunity to express your true feelings in a tangible way. And once you have written the words, they have an ongoing life of encouragement and comfort. The words can be read over and over again, cherished, and preserved with other mementos.

One common misconception about writing love notes is that you need to be a poet or skilled writer to create a love note to your spouse. That's just not true; anyone can do it! Here are some tips for writing an effective love note:

- ♥ *Stay off the word processor.* There is no replacing the handwritten note.

- ♥ *Be innovative.* Think about different and creative ways to express your feelings about your mate on paper. Don't just buy stock cards off the shelf. Instead, try making your own cards or note paper. Most stores carry a large supply of stickers and stamps; let your imagination run free. Or buy one of those "blank inside" cards and write your own custom-tailored message.

♥ *Be honest and sincere.* The point of an effective love note is not flattery, but positive communication. Put some effort into noticing your spouse's truly unique virtues and expressing appreciation for those traits.

♥ *Send a card through the mail.* The unexpected surprise of finding a note in the mail either at home or at the office may be just the thing to perk up your romance.

♥ *Don't wait for the special occasion to send a note.* Don't feel you need to wait for a holiday to celebrate. Make up your own holidays—like "I'm Glad We're Married Day" or your 2001th-day anniversary—or just celebrate being in love. Whatever you write, the unexpectedness will usually bring positive results.

Putting Some Fun in Your Time Together

Being married is not meant to be a burden. God created marriage to bring joy to each of us. So begin planning now to inject some fun back into your life together—on your dates or right in the middle of your everyday life. Go ahead; try something different. See if the following ideas can be a spark to rekindle the flame and excitement in your relationship:

(1) *The ABCs of love.* On one of your date nights, choose a letter of the alphabet to be your theme and customize your activities for the evening around it. For example, if your chosen letter was *A,* then you might choose to eat ambrosia at Alex's Diner. Later you might see the movie in Theater A in the local multiplex or visit the aquarium.

(2) *The love string.* Surprise your spouse after work one day by transforming your house into a maze—with you as the prize. Plan in advance for a friend to keep the children at their house. Tie a string to something near the entrance to your home with a note explaining that your spouse is to follow the string to the "love zone." Have the string wind throughout the house, with periodic instructions for what to do. Or place a gift at each point—perhaps a particular article of clothing! If your instructions are at all imaginative and your mate is at all persistent, the surprise at the end of the search will be worth the wait.

(3) *"I love you" coupons.* A felt-tip pen and some 3 x 5 cards are all you need to make your spouse feel loved and pampered. The coupons can be redeemable for a trip to the ice-cream parlor, a hot bubble bath, popcorn with a football game on TV, a foot rub—anything that spells fun or comfort to him or her.

(4) *The love jar.* This activity will require a little more work than the special coupons, but it can provide at least a year's worth of fun and romance. Go to a pharmacy and buy a box of empty medicine capsules. Then, on tiny strips of paper, write out some items or activities your spouse would enjoy doing or desire—for example:

- ♥ a back rub
- ♥ a movie date
- ♥ a picnic in the park
- ♥ a baseball game
- ♥ a day without the children
- ♥ fifty dollars to spend on new clothes
- ♥ flowers
- ♥ candy

Roll up the strips, put each in a separate capsule, and put all the "love capsules" in a jar. Present the jar to your spouse with a note instructing him or her to pull out a capsule as needed and "take as directed." (You might need to make arrangements in advance to make sure you can carry through on the activities listed.)

(5) *Let's make a date.* On a piece of cardboard, create a three-door game that will let your spouse select the place and price level of subsequent outings. Label the doors 1, 2, and 3. Behind each door, write the description of a particular date (for instance, "dinner at your favorite restaurant, followed by a night at the theater.") Behind another door may be a less extravagant date (such as "a fun-filled evening shopping for a new dress.") Behind the last door might be a "zonker." ("You've just won an exciting evening at home with two videos of your choice and a bowl full of popcorn.")

(6) *The portable restaurant.* You will need the help of some friends for this one. Find an unusual setting (a crowded shopping mall or the top of a building) or a romantic spot (ocean cliffs or a secluded lakeside location) and set up a table (a card table works nicely). Tell your spouse to dress up because you'll be going to a very nice place for dinner. Before you arrive at the "restaurant," arrange to have the table set with china and candles and friends dressed appropriately as waiters. As you eat, be sure to compliment the impeccable service and comment on the ambiance of the place.

Find a Mutual Recreational Activity

Early in your marriage (but it is never too late), determine a recreational activity you can enjoy together. Providing your spouse with a recreational partner can be a real gift. Think about what could fit for the two of you. It could be tennis, golf, hiking, jogging, biking, bowling, bird watching, stamp collecting—any of thousands of activities. If you are used to going your own ways, finding a common pursuit might take some effort. But the effort will pay large dividends in the quality of your relationship.

Pray Together

Praying together has added a wonderful richness to our marriage (Dave and Deb) and a new dimension to our prayer life. Praying out loud with your mate can help each of you keep focused and free from distractions. It also allows you to hear each other in intimate conversation with God. Your prayer time together does not have to be lengthy. It can consist of a few shared minutes before you go to bed or first thing in the morning. It does not even have to be daily; perhaps you could pray together on Saturday mornings while the children watch cartoons.

Read the Same Book

We have found that agreeing to read the same book as our spouse once in a while helps keep us disciplined to read as well as provides something we can talk about besides the house and the kids. What kind of book you read doesn't really matter; it can be anything from a novel to a nonfiction self-improvement book. The important part is that you are reflecting, discussing, and enjoying the same thing.

Set up a Love Calendar

This idea can really put some pizzazz into your life together. Get out a calendar and make plans to do something that communicates love to your spouse each day for a month. These daily expressions of love do not have to be expensive or time consuming; they can be as simple as an extra hug in the morning. What matters is that they be daily and premeditated.

Babysit for Your Spouse

Sometime the best way you can say "I love you" to your spouse will involve *not* being with him or her. Tell your spouse that you will watch the children for a period of time so that he or she can get way for some alone time.

Plan a Weekend Away

In addition to having your regular dates, you and your spouse need some extended time together. Try to get away for a weekend on a regular basis—just the two of you.

A weekend getaway will take some advance planning for most people; you will have to clear your calendar and make plans for taking care of the children. But the benefits make the effort worthwhile, even if you just spend it at a local campground or a budget motel.

Kidnap Your Spouse

The unexpected can add excitement and variety to your relationship. Plan out an evening or even a weekend getaway without telling your spouse where or what you are doing. Then pick him or her up at work or at home with bags packed, the gas tank full, and the babysitter on the way. Spirit your spouse off for a surprise outing.

Engineer a G.D.O.

Girls Day Out, which Deb and I (Dave) developed along with three other couples, is an advanced version of the weekend away and the kidnap getaway. What started as a fun day out together for the four couples has escalated into an extravagant weekend of romance. During the course of the year, the men get together several times in secret to plan the destination and schedule of the weekend—making sure that there is plenty of "alone time" for each couple as well as times when we all get together to talk and catch up on our friendships. We put aside money each month and take care of preparations so that when the appointed day arrives we are prepared to surprise, entertain, and seduce our wives in the proper fashion. A weekend like this takes a great deal of advance planning and creativity, but let me tell you—*it's worth it.*

///////// ♥ Marriages that Work ♥ /////////

A romantic and fulfilling marriage will take all the attention and love you have to give...and more. Unfortunately, if you are like us, you'll find plenty of reasons to be selfish. Maybe you'll feel too tired, or too busy, or even too angry to go out of your way to bring pleasure to your spouse. But the fact is, selfish people don't have great marriages. Marriage by its very nature takes effort, hard work, and an attitude that says "I'll be willing to meet your needs before I'll meet mine."

Work hard at doing those things that make your spouse feel good. Consider how your actions affect his or her self-image, confidence, and even physical well-being. Although this takes a concerted effort, we believe that the harder you work on keeping the romance in your marriage, the more enjoyable it will become for both of you.

///////////////////////////////// ♥ **ACTION STEPS** ♥ /////////////////////////////////

1. Discuss with your spouse which day of the week is best for a date night. Block out that night on your calendars for the next four weeks. Make the plans necessary to make the dates happen. Determine who is responsible for planning and preparing for which nights.

2. On a one-to-ten scale (ten means it cannot get any better, and one means it had better improve quickly or you will be in trouble), rate your relationship in the following critical areas:

Communicating with each other	1 2 3 4 5 6 7 8 9 10
Showing grace to each other	1 2 3 4 5 6 7 8 9 10
Giving encouragement to each other	1 2 3 4 5 6 7 8 9 10

3. If you scored below a seven in communicating, spend some time talking with your spouse. Try using a few of the "conversation starters" mentioned in this chapter.

4. If your score is below seven in showing grace, try doing a romantic calendar with an emphasis on doing gracious things for your spouse.

5. Trying one of the love-letter ideas is a good idea for you to try if you scored lower than seven on giving encouragement.

Maximum Family

// ♥

"Other things may change us, but we start and end with family."

—Anthony Brandt

"We know what a person thinks not by when he tells us what he thinks, but by his actions."

—Isaac Bashevis Singer

Several years ago, a research team from Oklahoma State University conducted an in-depth study of ninety-nine strong, healthy Oklahoma families, attempting to isolate the factors that made these families function so well. The results of that study were very interesting. According to the report, five factors began to emerge very early in the study. We believe these five factors give profound insight into what makes good family relationships:

1. Members of these families often expressed *appreciation* to each other.

2. These families spent a lot of time together. As a matter of fact, they intentionally cut down on the number of their outside activities and involvements in order to minimize the fragmentation of their family life.

3. They worked hard at keeping the lines of communication open and keeping their communication as positive as possible.

4. These strong families were devout. They were active in church as a family and, beyond that, regularly read the Bible and prayed together. But most important, they had a constant sense that God cared and was involved in the daily processes of their lives.

5. They were committed to the family, to spending time together, and to making each other happy.[1]

The research I (Charlie) did for my doctoral dissertation supports what I learned from the Oklahoma study. In my research I discovered that family management style has a direct relationship to the life satisfaction of the family members. As Dave and I looked at the results of my research and that of the Oklahoma team, we realized the qualities of healthy families could be grouped in two broad categories: *mutual support* and *decisive living*. The categories apply not only to the nuclear family, but to extended families and adoptive families as well.

Supporting
//////////////// ♥ One Another ♥ ////////////////

Mutual support is what happens when family members take an interest in the activities of the other family members. If one member is involved in a drama production or an athletic event, for instance, the entire family will attend the event together. Each member of the family would support the participating member in appropriate ways: applause, a smile, a pat on the back, a word of commendation.

We recently heard of a beautiful example of how one family member can support another. A teenaged girl was fighting the tendency to put on weight and so decided to jog a few miles every morning. Her father, however, felt it was dangerous for her to be out alone, so he volunteered to jog with her. For the next two years, father and daughter jogged together. Over that time, they became very close. They found time to discuss many subjects, and their joint activity helped keep the communication lines between them open. They now know each other to an extent that would not have been likely without the jogging. The memories they share will strengthen their relationship for years to come.

♥ Planning Life Together ♥

Strong family ties do not just leap into existence by themselves; they are built intentionally. And it is this process of "intentional building" that we call *decisive living*.

We recommend that husbands and wives sit down regularly to plan and ask themselves such questions as:

- ♥ "What is our family currently missing that would enrich us?"

- ♥ "What are we missing that we will later regret?"

- ♥ "Is either of us away from home too much?"

- ♥ "Are we doing some things that we can curtail in order to have more time together as a family?"

The answers to these questions may necessitate some changes for the whole family.

Decisive living involves more than asking hard questions. It also involves taking the time to build memories and relationships. It may even involve elaborate plans such as those made by a father we heard about recently.

This man, who really loved his family, had been planning a memorable summer vacation with them. At the last minute, however, the press of a business situation kept him tied to the office. Rather than cancel the trip, he insisted that his wife and kids go on the trip without him. They didn't want to go. In fact, they argued that they wouldn't. But in the end, dad prevailed.

The father helped his family plan every day of the camping trip. They would load up the family station wagon, drive to California, camp up and down the coast, then travel back home. Each day was carefully arranged. They were aware that their dad knew their whole route—the highways they would travel, the places they would stop, even the time they would cross the Great Divide. But it was what he didn't tell them that made the difference.

The father took off work (he'd planned it all along) and arranged to have himself flown to an airport near where his family would be on that particular day of the trip. He had also arranged to have someone pick him up and drive him to a place where every car on that route had to pass. With a wide grin, he sat on his sleeping bag and waited for that familiar station wagon packed full of kids and camping gear. When he spotted the station wagon, he stood up, stepped out onto the shoulder of the road, and stuck out his thumb.

Can you visualize that?

"Look! That guy looks like...Dad!"

The family had assumed he was a thousand miles away, sweating over a stack of papers. It's a wonder they didn't drive off into a ditch or collapse from heart failure. But they didn't. Instead, the picked up their father and proceeded on their way. Can you imagine the fun they had the rest of the trip? And the memories they stored away in their mental scrapbooks—could they ever be forgotten?

When he was later asked why he would go to all that trouble, the creative father replied, "Well, someday I'm going to be dead. When that happens, I want my wife and kids to say, "You know, Dad was sure a lot of fun." He will not only be known for having fun, but also for his *decisive living*.

Decisive living in families essentially means taking charge of the family's lives and making things happen. Too many families drift along at the mercy of whatever happens to them—good, bad, or indifferent. But if we want to experience a family environment that's good for all members, we need to make it happen!

Ideas to
///////////// ♥ **Make It Happen** ♥ /////////////

The following are some practical suggestions that will help you to create a healthy family environment that includes mutual support and decisive living. Remember that you cannot do everything, but you can do some things. And you definitely *can* have a family life with purpose.

Hugs and Kisses

Start while your family is very young with lots of hugs and kisses for everyone. Noted psychologist Virginia Satre and others have shown over and over again that people need to be touched. Dr. Satre states that people need:

- ♥ four hugs per day for survival,
- ♥ eight hugs for maintenance,
- ♥ and twelve hugs per day for growth.

One of the best things you can give to any member of your family is a hug and kiss. Two great things about a hug are that it is hard to give one without getting one in return and that in our busy, time-conscious society a hug still looks like a bargain. It takes only take a few seconds, and it is time well spent.

A Policy of Easy Access

This suggestion is for spouses and parents who are employed outside the home. The busier you are and the more time you spend away from family, the more important this little idea becomes. It involves giving out your private number at work to your family. If you don't have a private number, let your secretary or whoever answers the telephone know that family calls take priority. This policy of easy access goes a long way toward telling your spouse and children they truly have priority in your life. (If the rules of your workplace do not allow you this flexibility, your family will understand. The point here is to make family a priority when you make the choices that are available to you.)

A Nightly Blessing

A practice I (Charlie) started when my daughters were still in diapers was to put my hand on their head and pray a blessing on them every night as I tucked them into bed. It is a simple blessing: "Our Almighty and merciful God, Father, Son and Holy Spirit, bless Charlotte and Jana and keep them healthy and safe. Amen."

Once, when the girls were about five and eight years old, they told me with all seriousness that they didn't want a certain babysitter because she did not know the prayer. Even now, as teenagers, they seem to enjoy my hand and words of blessing before they go to sleep at night.

A Gift of Time

Several years ago, my wife and I (Charlie) decided to try a different approach to gift giving. Instead of giving the normal gifts of shirts, ties, and jewelry, we started giving the gift of time in the form of some type of activity. For example, we took my wife's dad out for a special deep-sea-fishing trip and her mother hot-air ballooning. For our youngest daughter, a Christmas shopping day with lunch included was an appreciated gift. We have found this kind of gift especially good for older children and senior adults.

A Gift of Your Presence

Events such as recitals, games, parties, camp-outs, performances, graduation, and exhibits at school are enhanced by your presence. Don't wait for the championship...for the big event. What might not seem important to you is important to your spouse and children. Don't miss the award banquets, even if your family member is not getting a major award.

My wife and I (Charlie) have watched many an athletic event, not because our daughter Jana was playing, but because she was cheering. I strongly suggest obtaining a copy of the school calendar or team schedule. Write all the important dates on both your family calendar and your personal calendar. Then make attending the events that are important to your family a priority in your life.

Making Special Events More Special

Your presence at special events is the most important way to lend support to those you love. With a little effort, however, you can also make these events even more special. Here are a few examples:

- ♥ *Celebrate with a special meal.* Going out for meal or letting the key person pick a favorite meal at home before a special event helps him or her feel special and supported.

- ♥ *Go out for dessert.* Going out for ice cream or other dessert—even to MacDonald's—after a recital, musical, or any event makes it extra special. Let the key person for the night pick the place.

- ♥ *Throw a party at home.* Inviting a few friends over for a party after a special event such as a graduation, special performance, or athletic competition demonstrates your support and love for your family. A decorated cake always enhances the occasion—and don't forget the balloons!

- ♥ *Plan a video party.* Videotape a special event. (If you don't have a video camera, you can probably rent or borrow one.) Then invite participants in the event over to watch the show. Popcorn is a nice touch. Videos of these special events will grow in sentimental value with each passing year.

Making the Most of Traditions and Holidays

Special days and family traditions provide great opportunities for quality time together. Let us suggest some examples that have enhanced our own family's lives:

- ♥ *Let Dad do the valentines.* On or around Valentine's day, have dad fix dinner for the family.

- ♥ *Head for the beach—or somewhere else that's great.* One of the highlights of each summer for us as a family when my children were small was renting a house at the beach for a week each summer. We all looked forward to those seven days of sand, sun, and togetherness. In a different part of the country, a trip to the mountains, the lake, or some other area of natural beauty could serve the same purpose.

- ♥ *Go camping.* The tradition of a father-son (or mother-daughter) camping trip, even if it starts in the backyard, can reap rich dividends of memories.

- ♥ *Work on a float.* For the past few years, we have enjoyed working on floats for the Rose Bowl parade. Almost every town has some type of parade or similar civic activity you can participate in together.

- ♥ *Minister together.* Several families I know have had their lives enriched by choosing to spend their holidays together in ministering to others. Try spending Thanksgiving serving food at a local rescue mission. Or if your children are small, consider having their Easter egg hunt at a nursing home. The residents will love watching the children hunt, and the whole family will benefit from reaching outside themselves.

♥ *Go on a Christmas walk.* In December, go out together walking or driving to see the Christmas lights. A special meal before or a dessert after would enhance the fun.

♥ *Participate in a living nativity.* Our church enacts a living nativity in front of the church each Christmas. Families sign up for thirty-minute spots as Mary, Joseph, shepherds, and other members of the nativity drama. Many families have made participation a family tradition. If your church doesn't do a nativity scene, you could even do your own in front of your house—or combine with a few other families to make it even more fun.

An Edification Calendar

A wonderful tool for decisive living is an edification calendar. To create one, get out your calendar and, for each day of the coming month, plan to do something that edifies (builds up) someone in your family. A day's activity could be anything from a pat on the back to a note of affirmation to a candy bar or bouquet of flowers. You don't have to do a lot. What matters is that you make a conscious, premeditated effort that says the other person is important to you.

Special Gifts for Special Occasions

Special occasions can be enhanced by special gifts. These do not need to cost a great deal of money; in fact, making them is better than buying them. Your family knows how important your time is, so your taking the time to make something means a lot. You can even special-order trophies and awards to recognize qualities you value in family members.

The Wall of Honor

Somewhere in your house—it could even be the refrigerator door when you have younger children—have a place to display special artwork, trophies, and plaques of recognition. Be sure to point out your wall of honor to visitors in your home.

Children's Night Out

Set up a tradition of taking your children out on a regular basis for an activity of their choice. Children's night out could involve anything from dinner at MacDonald's and miniature golf to a night at the ballet and a fancy dessert afterward. Work out a schedule that fits the number of children you have, your schedule, your spouse's desires, and your budget. But make it a scheduled event and make it a priority. If you start doing this when your children are young, you can carry the tradition through the teen years and maybe even into adulthood.

Sending Notes and Cards

Everyone loves to receive mail, and your family is no exception. Mail a note or card to different family members, telling them how much you love and appreciate them. Even little notes under their pillows or in their lunch boxes can be highly effective in communicating your support.

///// ♥ Maximum Family Now ♥ /////

We encourage you to be people of action where your family is concerned. Take steps now to make your family times memorable and special. Life is too short and relationships too precious to do otherwise. (It seems like only last week that our children were learning to walk, and now Charlie's youngest is learning to drive.) If you allow yourself to become too hurried to show love to your family, you may well find that love hurries by you. But we've never heard of anyone who has regretted spending too much time with friends and family.

The title of Frederick Speakman's book, *Love Is Something You Do,* is especially apt in this regard. Often we think of love as consisting of spectacular emotions and heroic acts. But in reality, such moments of intensity make up only a small part of our lives. Instead, the best relationships (with God, family, and friends) are built up like a fine lacquer finish, with accumulated layers made of many little acts of love. And like a lacquer finish, love grows more and more beautiful with each additional layer.

///////////////////////////////// ♥ **ACTION STEPS** ♥ /////////////////////////////////

1. We talked about the five patterns of a strong family:

appreciation
time together
communication
devotion
commitment

Circle each of the patterns you are currently acting out with your family. Put an *X* beside the one you are doing the best, and a check (√) beside the one (or two) you most need to work on as a family.

2. Sit down with your spouse and discuss the following questions:

   ♥ "What is our family currently missing that would enrich us?"

♥ "What are we missing that we will later regret?"

♥ "Is either of us away from home too much?"

♥ "Are we doing some things that we can curtail in order to have more time together as a family?"

3. Make a list of major family events coming up in the next nine months. Be sure that both husband and wife get the dates for those events on their calendars.

4. If your children are involved with sports, the arts, or some other organized activity, obtain a schedule of upcoming events and write the time and location of each event on your calendar. Do everything possible to be at as many games or performances as possible.

5. What one specific thing could you realistically do to give your family a greater feeling of support from you? Make the necessary plans to do it.

Closing Thoughts

/// ♥

We wrote *Too Hurried to Love* in the hope that it would change lives. And it has changed two lives already...our own.

In many ways, this book reflects our own struggle to manage demanding schedules and still find time to love God and the people who are most precious to us. Our goal from the beginning has not been to convince you that you have a problem—you probably already knew that, or you would not have bought the book in the first place. Our goal was to encourage you to live busy yet purposeful and fulfilled lives that bless God and the people you love. As you put this book down, let us encourage you to keep in mind a few simple thoughts:

(1) *Don't expect miracles overnight.* The process we have laid out for you is just that...a process. You are being perfected by God, but it is a slow process. The principles we've talked about and the practical applications we've suggested do work when you apply them consistently over a period of time.

(2) *Seek the Lord with your whole heart.* You will find that he will direct you and give you wisdom (see Prov. 3:5,6 and James 1:5). When seeking to discover a life direction and then to live it out, you must keep in mind that it is God who is ultimately in control of your destiny (see James 4:13-15).

(3) *Don't panic or burn this book when you fail.* Don't fall into the trap of thinking you're a failure as a person just because you have personal failings. You're only a failure when you've given up all hope and refuse to make any effort.

Chances are, you will fail from time to time. (Everyone does.) You'll probably have times when you find yourself slipping into a hurried lifestyle again or starting to skim in your relationships. Maybe you'll get off course and neglect your vital priorities. If that happens, don't worry. Making the principles of this book part of your lifestyle takes time and sustained effort. As time passes, you'll find that you'll be making decisions according to your stated life direction and priorities more and more.

(4) *Enjoy your life!* Have fun with what you do; be creative and even a little nutty with your relationships. Do some things that allow you to laugh and play together. The old Greek proverb is still true: "You will break the bow if you always keep it bent."

(5) *Share this book and its principles.* Now that you have realized the benefits of putting relationships first and living your life on purpose, why not let others in on what you've discovered? There are lot of "too hurried" people out there who would love to stop chasing the carrot...if they only knew how.

May God bless you as you commit yourself to a clear life direction and better relationships. Remember, he wants these things in your life as much as you do.

> These things I have spoken to you, that My joy may be in you, and that your joy may be made full. This is My commandment, that you love one another, just as I have loved you." (John 15:11,12 NASB)

Study Questions

// ♥

Chapter 1

1. When was the busiest time in your life? How long did it last?

2. What was fun about being that busy? What was bad?

3. To whom would you point as a person who modeled a workaholic work ethic for you as you were growing up? How influential was that person in your life?

4. To whom would you point as a person who manages to lead a focused and fairly balanced life? How has that person influenced you?

5. Reflect on the Erma Bombeck piece (p. 20-21) and write your own "If I could live my life over" list. What would you change about your life if you were given another chance? What would stay the same?

Chapter 2

1. In Philippians 4:12, the apostle Paul talks about learning the secret of being content in any situation. What do you think that secret is?

2. How would you describe your relationship with Jesus Christ? What difference does that relationship make in your life?

3. Henry Thoreau said that people "hit only what they aim at." If you had to mention one specific thing you are aiming for, what would it be?

4. If you had the power to change one thing in the world, what would it be? Why? Is there anything you can do now to make that change, even if in a small way?

5. What do you want people to say about you as your days come to an end? What are you currently doing to make people think that way about you?

Chapter 3

1. What do you think the opening quote by Alfred E. Newman means: "Most people don't know what they really want—but they're sure they haven't got it"?

2. In your opinion, what are the characteristics of a successful life? How do you know when you are successful?

3. When in your life did you feel the most successful? What were the circumstances?

4. Do you agree or disagree with Tom Peters' statement that you cannot have both a satisfying personal life and a successful professional life? Why?

5. Do you feel that people who have not learned how to serve can be truly happy? Why or why not?

6. What is your reaction to the Mr. Kimball-Billy Graham story? What does it say to you about your own life?

7. When in your life did you feel the most significant? What were the circumstances?

Chapter 4

1. In your personal experience, have you found that being best was a moving target? If you can, tell about a time when you discovered this to be true.

2. Have you ever felt used by someone who was trying to get to the top? What did you think about that person?

3. What can we learn from Harvard's Grant Study of Adult Development? Do you feel the findings from this study are valid? Can you think of instances from your own experience that seem to support or contradict the findings of the study?

4. What sort of things motivate you to do your personal best?

5. What hinders you from doing your best?

Chapter 5

1. What do you feel Frederick Buechner is saying when he states, "The trouble oftentimes with religious people is that they try to be more spiritual than God Himself"? Is that really possible?

2. What are some of the limits that can keep a person from doing it all? What limits have you come up against in your own life?

3. What are some principles of life management we can learn from Jesus' time on earth?

4. Under what circumstances do you find it most difficult to say no? Explain.

5. Have you learned some helpful techniques for successfully saying no? If so, what are they?

6. What insights about yourself or others did you gain from the parable about the animal school? Can you think of a real-life situation where those insights would apply?

Chapter 6

1. Describe what your "egg basket" of life currently looks like. What did it look like six months ago? What would you like for it to look like?

2. What sort of activities do you usually put on your calendar? What sort of activities do you think should be there?

3. In light of Proverbs 23:4,5, what part should money play in our decision concerning what we do with our time and energy?

4. Bill Cosby said, "I don't know the key to success, but the sure way to failure is to try to please everyone." What do you think he meant by that statement? Do you agree?

5. What does the concept of "wobble room" mean to you? Do you think it is a helpful concept? Why?

6. What have you discovered in your own life that puts you into "option overload"? Do you think this is a problem for most other people?

7. What have you discovered about yourself that helps keep you out of option overload? Do you think this idea can help other people?

Chapter 7

1. Do you think it is time in your own life for you to retreat for some alone time with God? If you are meeting together in a group, how can the other group members help make this happen? How do you think you will benefit from this time?

2. What book(s) have you read that have inspired you most in your relationship with God?

3. When can you remember hearing the voice of God? What was the setting? What message did you receive?

4. Is retreating alone with God as beneficial for you as going to church? Why?

5. Have you ever read someone's journal or diary? How did you feel?

6. If you currently keep a journal, share the benefits of doing so. If you don't...why not?

7. Which of the suggestions listed on pages 132–138 would you be willing to try this week?

Chapter 8

1. If you are meeting in a group, go around the circle and assign one of the ad slogans listed below to each person in the group. Which one would you choose for yourself?

   ♥ "Reach out and touch someone."

   ♥ "Things go better with _____."

   ♥ "Gentle but effective."

   ♥ "Everything you want and a little bit more."

   ♥ "Oh, what a feeling!"

   ♥ "When you care enough to send the very best."

   ♥ "You've come a long way, baby!"

   ♥ "The friendly skies."

   ♥ "Just one look, that's all it took..."

   ♥ "When _____ talks, people listen."

♥ "Let the good times roll."

♥ "Takes a lickin' and keeps on tickin'."

♥ "＿＿＿＿ has a better idea."

♥ "＿＿＿＿ tries harder."

♥ "I can't believe I ate the whole thing."

♥ "You're in good hands with ＿＿＿＿."

♥ "Put some snap, crackle, and pop in your life."

♥ "We treat you right."

♥ "Life is too short not to go first class."

2. What do you think are the four most important qualities of a true friend?

3. Which of your friends would you call first in a time of real need? Why that person or those persons?

4. Would you say that American society encourages friendships? Why or why not?

5. Do you think men seek qualities in friends that are similar to those women seek? In your experience, how do men's and women's friendships differ?

6. What would you add to the list of the benefits of friendship on pages 149-151.

Chapter 9

1. What would you list as the most romantic thing your spouse has ever done for you?

2. Read aloud Walter Trobisch's words on page 159 and then read 1 Corinthians 13 from the Bible. What characteristics of love do you believe need to be learned?

3. What factors keep most couples from meaningfully communicating with one another? What creative ways can you come up with to help others with this problem?

4. Which of the ideas for dates listed in this chapter (or picked up from other group members as they shared their answers to question 1) would you like to try on your date with your spouse this week?

5. Spend a few minutes writing down ten reasons why you love your spouse. After you've both finished, turn toward each other and read your list quietly to one another.

Chapter 10

1. What do you remember about bath time as a child? What do those memories tell you about the quality of the family life you experienced as a child?

2. What would you list as the main aspects of your current family life that make for good relationships?

3. What do you enjoy most about your family right now?

4. What most frustrates you about the current state of your family life?

5. What specific actions are you currently taking to "live decisively" as far as your family is concerned? What are some things you would like to do?

Notes

Chapter 1

1. Associated Press dispatch, *Tacoma News Tribune,* 29 March 1990.
2. George Barna *The Frog in the Kettle: What Christians Need to Know About Life in the Year 2000* (Ventura, CA: Regal, 1990), 39.
3. Janice Castro, "The Simple Life," *Time,* 8 April 1991, 62.
4. Erma Bombeck

Chapter 2

1. Janice Castro, "The Simple Life," *Time,* 8 April 1991, 62.
2. Amy Saltzman, *Downshifting: Reinventing Success on a Slower Track,* mentioned in Elizabeth Venant, "Hard Pressed to Have Fun," *Los Angeles Times.*
3. R. Alec MacKenzie, *The Time Trap* (New York: McGraw-Hill, 1972), 38.
4. Quoted in Don J. McMinn, *Strategic Living* (Grand Rapids, MI: Baker, 1988), 154.
5. Gail Sheehy, *Pathfinders* (New York: William Morrow, 1981), 264.
6. Sheehy, *Pathfinders,* 45.
7. Viktor E. Frankl, *Man's Search for Meaning* (Boston: Beacon, 1939, 1963), 122.
8. William H. Mikesell, *The Higher Purpose* (Anderson, IN: Warner Press, 1961), 79.
9. Frankl, *Man's Search,* 104.
10. Frankl, *Man's Search,* 210.
11. Quoted in Tim Hansel, *Holy Sweat* (Waco, TX: Word, 1987), 81.

Chapter 3

1. Gordon MacDonald, *Ordering Your Private World* (Nashville: Oliver Nelson, 1984), 191.

2. Jack Horn, "Trading Up," *Psychology Today,* October 1988, 20.
3. David Ogilvy, *Confessions of an Advertising Man* (New York: Athenaeum, 1980).
4. Tom Peters and Nancy Austin, *A Passion for Excellence* (New York: Random House, 1985), 117.
5. Harold Kushner, *When All You've Ever Wanted Isn't Enough* (New York: Summit Books, 1986), 18.
6. Quoted in Hansel, *Holy Sweat,* 144.
7. Quoted in Hansel, *Holy Sweat,* 159.
8. Janice Castro, "The Simple Life," *Time,* 8 April 1991, 58–59.
9. Not her real name.

Chapter 4

1. "In Praise of the Conventional Life," *Forbes,* 17 October 1988, 157–58.
2. Bertrand Russell, *The Conquest of Happiness,* quoted in Stan J. Katz and Aimee E. Liu, *The Success Trap* (New York: Ticknor & Fields, 1990), 188.

Chapter 5

1. Sybil Stanton, "Bionic or Bust," in Sybil Stanton, *The 25 Hour Woman* (New York: Bantam, 1986).
2. Judith Viorst, "Self Improvement Program," in *How Did I Get to Be 40 and Other Atrocities* (New York: Simon and Schuster, 1976), 45.
3. Flora Davis, "How to Live with Stress and Thrive," *Woman's Day,* 22 May 1979, 78.
4. Covert Bailey, *Fit or Fat* (Boston: Houghton Mifflin, 1977), 23.
5. Harold Begbie, *Life of General William Booth* (New York: Macmillan, 1920), 178.
6. M. Scott Peck, *The Road Less Traveled* (New York: Simon & Schuster, 1978), 64.
7. C.S. Lewis, *Letters to an American Lady* (Grand Rapids, MI: Eerdmans, 1975), 53.

Chapter 6

1. Chris Dufresne, "Well Worth the Wait," *Los Angeles Times,* 19 January 1991, C-1, C-12.
2. Dennis Wholey, *Discovering Happiness* (New York: Avon, 1988), 266.

Chapter 7

1. Mrs. Charles E. Cowman, *Springs in the Valley* (Minneapolis: Worldwide, 1939, 1980), 75.

2. Ben Patterson, *The Grand Essentials* (Waco, TX: Word, 1987), 125.
3. Adapted from Em Griffin, *Getting Together* (Downers Grove, IL: Inter-Varsity, 1982), 98.

Chapter 8

1. Rollo May

Chapter 9

1. Walter Trobisch, *Love Is a Feeling to Be Learned* (Downers Grove, IL: InterVarsity Press, 1972), 6.

Chapter 10

1. *Family Strength,* Fall 1976, 6–8.